Asset Protection
Pure Trust Organizations

Copyright © 2011
by David E. Robinson

First Edition, October, 2011

This information is offered for educational purposes only; not to be taken as legal advice.

All Rights Reserved
Parts of this book may be reproduced subject to due and specific acknowledgment of their source.

MAINE-PATRIOT.com
3 Linnell Circle
Brunswick, Maine 04011

maine-patriot.com

Pure Trust Organizations 1

Asset Protection

"God gives you His ideas, and they in turn give you daily supplies."

Asset Protection
Pure Trust Organizations
Contents

APPENDIX

Asset Protection

Introduction
Advantages of a Pure Trust

Knowledge is the power of the Global Community.

For those who consider confidentiality vitally important.

Trusts offer Privacy, Protection, Profit.

A Trust provides the first step toward total privacy. With a Trust, the Trust can conduct banking anywhere in the world. International Banking provides the most ideal method for receiving profits, but only through a Trust.

What can this do for you?

1. Assets are protected 100% — the #1 enemy in the world is litigation.
2. Protection from creditors.
3. Protection from liability suits.
4. Protection from malpractice suits.
5. Protection from employees.
6. Protection from personal bankruptcy.
7. Protection from excessive divorce settlements.
8. Avoids probate.
9. Avoids inheritance tax.
10. Avoids estate taxes.

11. Avoids court actions.

12. Eliminates attorney fees.

13. Eliminates or reduces Accountant fees.

14. Eliminates Executor's fees.

15. Eliminates or reduces Income taxes.

16. Frees tax dollars for capital appreciation.

17. Provides complete control over your assets through trustees.

18. No public record.

19. Ownership and title can be passed to heirs in complete secrecy.

20. Trust is perpetual — The Trust lives on continuously.

21. Heirs cannot change, challenge, or contest any wishes at your passing-on.

22. The Trust is easy to maintain and very inexpensive.

1
Principles of Trusts

"The people perish for lack of Knowledge." — *Hosea 4:6.*

"No state shall pass any bill of attainder, ex post facto law, or law impairing the obligation of contract." — *The Constitution of the United States, Article 1, Section 10.*

"The citizens of each state shall be entitled to all privileges and immunities of citizens in several states." — *The Constitution of the United States, Article 4, Section 2, Clause 1.*

The properly structured Pure Trust Organization provides the quickest and simplest legal road to freedom, creating the ultimate in tax immunity and iron clad asset protection! By transferring assets into properly structured and legally recognized Pure Trust Organizations, you are able to maintain complete control of all the benefits of asset ownership, without the inherent liabilities.

Because the assets are "held in trust", they cannot be liened, seized, or levied for the debts of the trustees or its beneficiaries. Further, the trustees and the beneficiaries are not liable for the debts of the Pure Trust.

American Citizens have the unlimited freedom to hold, transfer, sell, or dispose of their property in any manner they desire. It is neither unethical nor unlawful to intelligently protect your family's property and your family to legally and intelligently preserve what you have worked a lifetime to obtain.

Pure Trust Organizations have been utilized by wealthy financially sophisticated Americans for hundreds of years. Transferring assets into a properly structured Pure Trust Organization is as easy as transferring property to another person. Assets can be conveyed into a trust even if an erroneous Notice of Lien has been filed against the property.

As confirmed by the Chief of Accounting of the IRS, "A Pure Trust has no tax requirements." Therefore there are no legal requirements for a Pure Trust Organization to file a tax return.

"Since the business trust has its origin in the common-law right of the parties to enter into contract, and does not spring from a franchise granted by the state, it has been held that the constitutional authority to levy excises upon commodities (income tax), a term including corporate franchises, does not empower the legislature to impose an excise (privilege) tax on business trusts." — *266 Mass 590, 163 NE 904, 63 ALR 192.*

The courts ruled that a Pure Trust is not illegal even if formed for the express purpose of reducing or avoiding taxes. — *13 Am Jur 2nd '85, In Weeks' v. Sibley D.C. 269 F, 155, Edwards v. Commissioner, 415 F2d 578,582 10th Cir. (1969)* and *Phillips v. Blatchford, 187 Mass 510.*

The courts ruled that persons may adopt any lawful means for the lessening of the burden of income taxes. — *Edison California Stores, Inc. v. McColgan, 30 Cal 2nd 372, 183 P2d 16.*

"Avoidance of Taxes is not a criminal offense." — *The Department of the Treasury IRS Handbook for Special Agents #4112: Tax avoidance Distinguished from Evasion.*

Any attempt to reduce, avoid, minimize, or alleviate taxes by legitimate means is permissible."

"It is not an evasion of legal responsibility to take what advantages may accrue from the choice of any particular form of organization permitted by law." — *Narragansett Mut. F. Ins. Co., v. Burnhamn, 51 R 1372, 154 A 909.*

Never in the history of America, has the need for property and asset protection been greater. It is a stark reality in today's world that a sudden financial reversal, an unanticipated lawsuit, or the stroke of a bureaucrat's pen, can, overnight, wipe out a lifetime of accumulated savings and assets.

Regulatory assaults on probate property are at an all time high. Under recently passed Asset Forfeiture Laws, the government can seize probate property for minor third party offenses of which the property owner may not even be aware. This can create costly legal expenses and tie up time in court, even if the owner is innocent.

The Pure Trust Organization is a powerful tool, which can be used to protect a Citizen's property from the myriad of regulatory abuses, imposed by the government as well as frivolous law suites.

Also, in today's computed and technological super communication age, your privacy can be invaded with the stroke of a keyboard. With a Citizens' social security number or federal ID#, personal information can easily be discovered that can fraudulently be used to abuse their credit and misappropriate their assets. Because the Pure Trust Organization is lawfully established and bank accounts are opened in a fictitious name without a social security or federal identification number, paper trails to the Citizen are permanently severed.

Most Americans do not realize that they have a choice of laws when conducting their personal and/or business affairs. Rarely do we hear about the legally recognized American common law which is the "people's laws", created by and for them.

The common law existed long before statutory law and is as viable today as it was in the beginning of our country's history. Originally the common law was created to protect the rights and the property of the people against the abuses of the sovereign king. Unfortunately today, the common law trust is seldom utilized to protect the people's property against the abuses of our current government. In America the people are sovereign and may choose to legally conduct their affairs outside of government regulation, under the common law.

Statutory law is a creation of the government for the purposes or regulating, fining, and penalizing the people. Although it is in the best self-interest of attorneys, CPAs and the government to promote statutory trusts, which are a "creature of the legislature", and therefore have stringent regulatory and tax requirements, this type of trust is the most inhibiting for the Citizen.

Statutory Trusts provide only limited protection for property and a truckload of paperwork and taxes for the Citizen. The Statutory Trust is referred to as a "Revocable Living Trust" or "Grantor Trust", and is required to file a 1041 Form every year. Whereas the common law, in American, is law based upon the principles of justice and reason.

Under the common law, as long as Citizens do not infringe upon the rights of others and keep all agreements entered into "knowingly, intentionally, and voluntarily", they are absolutely free to legally conduct their lives and/or businesses in any manner they choose.

Under the common law, an American Citizen cannot be compelled to do anything against his/her consent.

The common law trust, being a creature of our constitutional right to contract, has no government regulations, no tax liability and is not legally required to file a tax return. To put it simply, the Internal Revenue Service and other agencies of the government have NO JURISDICTION over common law Pure Trust Organizations. It is American free enterprise in its purest form!

Asset Protection

2
Financial Planning for the Future

The knowledgeable and wealthy have continued to utilize the pure trust throughout American history.

When the original thirteen colonies won their independence, the man who was reputed to be the richest in the nation, William Bingham, who also served as a Senator from Pennsylvania in the 2nd United States Congress, started a pure contract trust for his estate, which, at one time, held over two million acres in Maine.

After 160 years of operation, the trust was terminated in 1964 upon the sale of the last of the properties involved, and because the number of beneficiaries had grown to over 300. During the trust's existence, however, it was not affected by the death of its creator or by the death of generations of trustees. It never paid a cent in probate costs or estate (death) taxes.

The Kennedy family is known to maintain a number of pure trusts, a process which was begun when Joseph Kennedy created a pure trust to own the Chicago Merchandise Mart, which was valued according to a *Chicago Tribune* article dated March 22, 1947, at some $30 million dollars.

William Waldorf Astor, saving his heirs millions of dollars in probate costs and estate taxes, created a $50 million dollar trust estate. It is reported that when John D. Rockefeller died, he had over 250 pure trusts. Rumor has it that the number of Rockefeller pure trusts now tops the 2,000 mark.

The billion-dollar-plus Mellon family (Mellon Bank) has extensively utilized a complex structure of Pure Trust Organizations. The *Dallas Morning News* carefully researched the estate of Texas oil man H.L. Hunt who died with less than $30,000 in total personal assets (automobiles valued at $21,250 dollars, plus $5,443 dollars on deposit in his name in the bank), yet, he passed complete control of an estate estimated at two to five billions of dollars to his son, Bunker Hunt, without estate taxes or probate costs, through the use of pure trust organizations.

Why are we not utilizing the successful history of the knowledgeable and wealthy? The leading reason people are missing out on the best in trusts is because the majority have done nothing in preparing to leave assets to their children. Most people feel that they have plenty of time and will eventually do what needs to be done.

There are those who believe a good "will" is all they need. Their lawyer "friend" has convinced them that a will is the best option. There is no law that states that an estate has to go through probate, but a "will" *mandates* probate.

Years ago, knowing that there was no way to stop trusts from being used, lawyers arranged the legal system to where, if you used a "will", or made no provision for distribution of your estate, then the estate had to go through probate. "Wills" were then promoted and trusts were ignored until the last ten years or so.

3
Tax-free Living

A family utilized a trust and transferred its assets — including house, car, and equipment used in the family business (a farm) — to the trust.

The Family then entered into an employment contract with the trust, which required family members to live in their former house because their presence was required at all hours to manage the trust.

The trust agreed to pay the family's living expenses, including lodging and food. The family took the payments tax-free because the arrangement benefited their employer, and the trust deducted its expenses.

IRS Ruling: The arrangement is proper even if it was adopted with the explicit intention of avoiding taxes. — Source: *Letter Ruling 9134002.*

Asset Protection

4
Pure Trust Definitions

The Corpus

The property held within the Pure Trust is called the "corpus". One or more "trustees" manage the "corpus" for the benefit of an unlimited number of "Beneficiaries-Capital Unit Holders".

The Exchanger (or Settlor)

The Pure Trust is implemented after it has been signed and executed by all parties to the contract and the "Exchanger", who is also called a "Settlor", conveys property into it, creating the corpus of the trust, in *exchange* for "capital units". This constitutes a tax-free exchange. The "Exchanger" can hold all capital units or divided them among Beneficiaries of the Exchanger's choice. The Exchanger (Settlor) can be a Beneficiary-Capital Unit Holder or only a Capital Unit Holder.

Beneficiaries-Capital Unit Holders

Capital Units represent 100% of the "rights to the proceeds" and the "rights to the benefits" of the property held in the trust. This is called the "beneficial interest". This means that although the Exchanger no longer owns the property, he retains the benefits. For example, if a car is in the trust, the Beneficiary can drive the car. If a house is in the trust, he can sign a lease agreement with the trust and continue to live in the house. If a business is operating as a Pure Trust Organization, the Beneficiary-Capital Holder(s) have the right to the profits and proceeds of the business, etc.

The "Beneficiaries" of the Trust are "Capital Unit Holders". A Beneficiary-Capital Unit Holder has no management control of the Trust. Management control is the responsibility of the Trustee(s). For this reason, the trust is said to be "Pure", and the Beneficiary-Capital Unit Holder(s) are not liable for any obligations incurred by the trustees or managers appointed by the trustees.

The Trustees

The Trustees do not own the property held in the corpus by the Pure Trust Organization. They merely hold the property and manage it for the Beneficiary-Capital Unit Holder(s).

Pursuant to *Hussey v. Arnold, 70 NE 87; Mayo v. Moritz, 24 NE 1083,* even though the trustees hold property, that does not mean that the trustee(s) own the property. Trust property cannot be held under an attachment nor sold for the execution of any Trustee's debts. Trustees cannot be held liable for debts incurred by the trust.

The trustees cannot, in addition, be Beneficiary-Capital Unit Holder(s), but they can be paid and receive compensation for their function as Trustees.

Status of the Pure Trust Organization (PTO)

The "Pure Trust Estate" is irrevocable. This is not as intimidating as it sounds. A Pure Trust can buy, sell, or transfer property, into and out of the Pure Trust estate, like any other form of business, but you cannot move the property back and forth between you and the Trust if it is to be Pure. This is to your advantage because you would not want a crooked creditor to take you to court in order to force you to revoke the trust so that he can attach your property.

Transferring Property

Transferring property into a Contract of Trust is as simple as transferring it to any other third party. Property is simply transferred from the original owner to the *name of the trust.*

5
Structuring the Pure Trust

General Structure of the Pure Trust

The Pure Trust is like any other person or business entity, that has the power to hold, sell, or transfer property, conduct business, etc. It is simply an entity that has a different name, and ID number, than you. Property is transferred into the Name of the Pure Trust as if it were any other person.

Once title to the property is in the Name of the Trust Organization, it is protected by the ironclad contractual and constitutional protections contained in the trust instrument (document). Because your right to contract cannot be impaired, you have peace of mind in knowing that the property is safely protected. You will have the advantages of property ownership without the possible liabilities.

Number of Pure Trust needed for maximum Asset Protection

To maximize the benefits, of the Pure Trust Organization, it is vital to put each asset that has the *potential* for creating a liability into its own separate Pure Trust Organization so that it does not jeopardize other assets. In a lawsuit, lien, levy, etc., the only assets that can be seized are those assets that are held in the name of the person or entity *that created the liability.*

For example, let's say that your car was involved in a

serious accident that created a million dollars worth of damages and the insurance company refused to honor your claim. Because your name was on the Title to the car, if you are successfully sued, a judgement would be entered *in your name.* Therefore, every asset held *in your name* would be subject to seizure. *A Pure Trust allows you to contractually move assets out of your name,* while still retaining full control and all of the benefits of the property.

In the previous example, if you had had the forethought to put the Title to the car in the name of a Pure Trust, instead of in your name, only the Pure Trust could be sued, under its fictitious name. The assets held in your name or in the names of other trusts would be immune from judgement. If a court judgement, lien, or levy has been filed against you *personally,* only those assets that you hold *in your own name* are subject to seizure.

Businesses should always have a minimum of several Pure Trusts. **The first operating entity should hold beneficial interest of other trusts.** Other Pure Trusts should then be established under different names to hold and protect all other assets of the business organization. Business property and equipment that has the potential of creating a liability should always be segregated into separate trusts.

Naming the Pure Trust
Unless you are creating a Family Trust, do not use your last name or the word "Trust". **Name your business as if it were a Sole Proprietorship.** This will protect your privacy and will also make doing business and transferring property simpler.

The Trust Identification Number

Because a Pure Trust has no tax requirements, it has no need for a Federal Employer Identification Number or a Social Security Number, which are necessary for tax reporting purposes only.

The Pure Trust will be issued a nine-digit, internally generated, identification number for banking and identification purposes, unrelated to taxes. The Trust Identification Number is private and will not be linked to any Federal or State Government agency. It will be included on your final Pure Trust Document(s). Each Trust will be issued a separate number.

Naming Trustees and Beneficiaries

The most important rule to remember when structuring your Pure Trust is that you cannot be both a Beneficiary-Capital United Holder and a Trustee at the same time. It is the complete separation of these two entities, Beneficiary and Trustee, that affords the Pure Trust its protections. If the same person who holds the legal and equitable title, also has the beneficial interest or the right to proceeds, no trust has been created. The entity is then said to be operating as an "alter-ego" or as a "nominee" of the trust.

The Protector

The Protector has the power to terminate Trustees and-or appoint new Trustees. The Protector may also appoint "Successor Trustees" in the evet that a Trustee dies. A Protector cannot have any other position in the Pure Trust. A Protector can be anyone, related to or unrelated to you.

Trustees

Trustees hold the legal and equitable title to the property in Trust, for the benefit of the Beneficiaries-Capital Unit Holders. They do not, however, actually *own* the property. A Trustee cannot also be a Beneficiary-Capital Unit Holder. Trustees have no rights to the "beneficial interest" in the form of income and profits. However, they can receive a contractually agreed upon compensation in return for their Trustee services. Trustees have Management Control of the Pure Trust. There can be one Trustee or as many Trustees as desired. All of the Trustees can work together in managing the property, open and operate bank accounts, and take care of the day to day operations of the Trust.

Adversarial (Unrelated) Trustees

In order to maintain the tax immunity qualities of the Pure Trust, it is important that it is not considered a "Grantor" Trust, which is required to file a 1041 Form. According to the IRS: "The title of 'grantor trust' arises when there is no trustee with adverse interest." The words "adverse" or "adversarial" mean unrelated. The rule of structure is that "the majority of trustees must have an interest 'adverse' or unrelated to that of the beneficiaries-capital unit holders. This means that if the beneficiaries are your wife-husband-children, the *majority* of trustees cannot be related to them. Therefore, for example, if you were a man and wanted to be a trustee and make your wife and children beneficiaries, you must also have at least three other unrelated Trustees. These Trustees will delegate the authority to your Managing Trustee to open the bank account, sign checks, transfer property, sign the minutes and make management decisions concerning the contract of trust. If you are not related to the beneficiary(ies) you do not need adversarial trustees.

The Managers

Typically the manager will be responsible for the management of the Trust. The Manager is merely an employee of the Pure Trust and is not an integral part of it. However, some individuals choose this position because they want to manage the Trust with privacy. When transferring title to real property and automobiles, it is necessary to include the name(s) of the Trustee(s) in addition to the name of the Pure Trust, as a matter of public record. The Manager's name, however, would not appear on the title. It would only be included within the trust minutes, which are totally private.

The Beneficiary-Capital Unit Holders

Beneficiaries-Capital Unit Holders have the right to the "beneficial interest" which is a right to the income, profits, and proceeds and use of the Pure Trust Organization. However, in order to provide maximum asset protection, the trust must be "Pure".

The Trustee assigns capital units, which represent 100% of the beneficial interest of the Pure Trust, to the "Exchanger" (Settlor), in exchange for the property he or she conveys into the trust. The Exchanger can then either keep all Certificates or divide them in any manner among Beneficiaries of his or her choice.

Bank Accounts

A Pure Trust can open a completely private bank account at a major bank with no Federal ID or Social Security number. This account will be like any other checking account, except that it will be completely private.

Illustration

To establish a Pure Trust, you (the Exchanger) must exchange the title to your property (your house, your car, your business, etc.) designated in Capital Units, and $25 dollars weight of silver, offered, received, and accepted in hand, as consideration, with the Creator-Protector of the Trust, for 100% beneficial interest in the Trust.

It's a tax free equal value for equal value exchange.

The Creator-Protector will then create an irrevocable Pure Trust, and appoint you to be the Director-Trustee of the trust

You will then designate a Successor to direct the Trust, in the event of your incapacity, and appoint an adverse (unrelated) Trustee or Trustees, whom the Protector will have power to employ or discharge, to manage the Trust for the Beneficiary (s) of your choice.

— — —

The Protector cannot have any other position in the Pure Trust, but he can be anyone outside the Pure Trust.

The Managing Trustee can open a bank account in the Name of the Pure Trust.

If the Beneficiary(s) are related to a Trustee, the majority of Trustees must be adversary (unrelated) Trustees.

6
Questions & Answers
Re: Pure Trust Organizations

Q: *What are Pure Trust Organizations?*

A: A PTO is an entity formed by a contract that is capable of conducting any lawful business activity or operation, such as buying, selling, and holding property, etc. PTO's are governed according to the Common Law of Contracts and are created by citizens exercising their unalienable (literally, in-a-lien-able) rights, as recognized by the Declaration of Independence (1776) and Article 1, Section 10, of the Constitution for the United States of America (1787), which forbids our government from making any law which "impairs the obligation of contracts."

Unlike "statutory trust" entities (such as the strawman) which are subject to governmental regulation and taxation because they are created, registered, and regulated according to changeable congressional and state legislation, a pure trust organization is "pure" because it is untainted by outside influences. It is formed as a matter of a natural-born human's sovereign, unalienable right to contract, a right which, again, may not be impaired in any way by governmental interference, regulation, or taxation.

The contract creating the PTO becomes its own law — the only law to which the PTO is subject. Not even the name given a PTO upon its creation must be registered with or approved by any governmental entity, no matter how many other entities may share the same name.

Statutes that require persons or partnerships transacting business under a fictitious name to file a certificate giving the names and addresses of those making use of such name do not apply to business trusts that are, in their nature, pure trusts and not partnerships. — *National City Finance Co. v. Lewis, (Cal App) 3 P2d 316, reh dent (Cal App) 4 P2d 163, and Gen'l Amer. Oil v. Wagoner Oil & Gas.*

Business entities (sole proprietorships, partnerships, limited liability companies, joint ventures, corporations, and all but one type of trust organization) derive their recognized form of existence from and through government, whereas the pure trust organization does not.

Because it is an entity created by sovereigns exercising their natural, unalienable right to contract, it is not subject to governmental interference in any form.

Q: *How do PTO's work?*

A: **Step 1: You** as **Founder-Trustor** of a desired PTO contract with a **Creator-Protector** for an exchange of property in return for the right to the final disposition of assets when and if the PTO is ever dissolved. This contract involves a *quid pro quo* equal value for equal value exchange.

Step 2: Through the process of the exchange, the **Creator-Protector** assigns **your property** to a fictional legal entity called a PTO. In the exchange, **you offer and receive** $25 dollars of silver, as consideration for 100% of the right to the final distribution of the assets of the PTO when and if it is ever dissolved.

Step 3: The **Creator-Protector** will then **appoint and employ you** to to be the **Managing Trustee** of the PTO to administer the affairs of the PTO according to the terms of the contract. This **Creator-Protector** must be someone not related to you by blood, marriage, or cohabitation.

Step 4: You then designate the **Beneficiaries** of the trust.

Q: *Why should $25 dollars in silver be part of the exchange?*

A: Many people transfer assets to some entity for protection from taxation only to have the IRS come back and set aside the transfer because "valuable consideration" did not take place.

Under the America's Constitution, valuable consideration occurs when the value in consideration is in excess of twenty (20) dollars of lawful money. When the value in consideration exceeds this amount there is the right to a trial by jury in the event of a dispute (something not available in tax court).

Note: As many of your know, the only "lawful money" in the United States are coins minted in silver of gold. This is specified in the original Constitution of 1787, as well as in the current laws of the United States (31 USC 5112). The paper currency that we use are "Federal Reserve Notes" and say on their face: — "This note is legal tender for all debts public and private. Before silver coins were withdrawn from general circulation in the 1960's, they used to read, "This note is legal tender for all debts public and private and is redeemable in lawful money"; but, in 1966, Congress passed the Federal Tax Lien Act. On page 3722 of that law, in a section subtitled "Legislative History", Congress wrote these words: "The entire taxing and monetary systems of the United States are hereby placed under the Uniform Commercial Code." This allowed "lawful money" to be totally withdrawn from circulation and replaced with "legal tender". Under the UCC, there are four types of legal tender: Cashier's checks, Money Orders, Certificates of Deposit, and Promissory Notes, but none of these is "lawful money".

Q: *What is an EIN?*

A: Most natural-born Americans choose to obtain (they believe that they are required to obtain) a Social Security Number (SSN) from the Social Security Administration. The IRS also uses this number for identification purposes. If this number is obtained from the IRS instead of the Social Security Administration, as is sometime the case, it is referred to as a Taxpayers Identification Number (TIN).

An Employer Identification Number (EIN) is a number that the IRS assigns to business entities, non-profit organizations, and public institutions-agencies that have tax requirements, employees, and an obligation to pay income or payroll-related taxes and file reports with the IRS concerning those taxes. It's primarily used on tax returns and other reports with the IRS.

Q: *What "tax requirements" are currently being imposed on business entities, non-profit organizations, and public institutions-agencies?*

A: There are several, as follows:

1. The requirement to pay "income taxes" on "income (profit) or "capital gains".

2. The requirement to report on the distribution of income (profits) to others, such as sole proprietors, partners, shareholders, and beneficiaries.

3. The requirement to account for and pay to the IRS sums that were withheld (for income tax, Social Security, and Medicare) from the salaries and wages of employees.

4. The requirement to account for an pay employer "matching" contributions, such as Social Security and Medicare Insurance, for those employees who are participating in these programs.

5. The requirement to account for and pay other "employee taxes", such as federal unemployment insurance.

Q: *Why doesn't a pure trust organization have tax requirements?*

A: PTO's have no tax requirements because they are sovereign entities, having been established as such under English common law and through the 200-plus years of American jurisprudence. "Sovereigns" are not subject to taxation or regulation. "Subjects" are.

If we look at the history of trusts, this distinction becomes clearer. Trusts were a part of ancient Hebrew law. Around 400 BC, Plato used a trust to create a "sovereign" university in Greece. Trusts were also a part of Roman law. Jesus scolded the religious elite of his day for making a big show of generously pledging their assets upon death as a gift to the temple (a form of trust agreement that we'd call a "charitable remainder trust") and then using that as an excuse for their private stinginess in not generously caring for their elderly parents.

Trusts were used as early as the 11th century in the English-speaking world. By the 1400's, they were being enforced by the Courts of Chancery. The basis in English written law, however, dates to the Magna Carta of 1215 when knights who were weary of having the king take their lands when they went off to war persuaded King John to make this famous document. He wasn't happy about signing it because, until then, he was the only recognized sovereign in the land. But given the alternative of being beheaded if he didn't sign it, he saw the wisdom in recognizing that **Man** (Knights, not common man-serfs) **is sovereign. Sovereigns can own land and are not "subject" to taxation** — "Subjects" pay taxes.

Common law trusts were soon established. **Knights could choose to have their estates held by a separate party,** such as a friend, or the church.

Property would be held "in trust" for the knight and his family. If the knight didn't return from battle, his family wasn't put out of house and home. The knight may have died, but the trust (as its own entity) did not die. If a knight was foolish enough not to put his property and estate in trust, many burdens would fall on the holder of legal title. For instance, if the son of the former owner was still a minor, the King had a right to claim fees. Also, if a property owner was ever convicted of a crime, he world forfeit all that he owned to the king, leaving his family in poverty. Trusts had many other advantages, as well, including privacy.

You may recall that the Revolutionary War was motivated, in large part, by what was perceived as oppressive taxation of the American Colonies by the King of England and by the "swarms" of agents sent to tax and harass the American people. In pursuing and establishing independence from the King of England, the American revolutionaries established that the sovereignty formerly held by the King (and by Lords, Dukes, and Knights) belongs to We the People — to each of us, individually, since "we are endowed by our Creator with unalienable rights" and to all of us, collectively, who joined together to form "a more perfect union" of sovereign, independent republic states in which we reside as free, independent, sovereign citizens.

Patrick Henry was a patriot whose passionate phrasing, "I know not what course other men may take; but, as for me, give me liberty, or give me death!" inspired many during the days before the Revolutionary War. One day, Mr. Henry was approached by Robert Morris, Governor of the Virginia Colony and a man who became a prominent financier of the American Revolution. Morris requested that Patrick Henry establish a trust for his property. King George was taxing property owned by any English subject, but he couldn't tax land owned by a sovereign or by a pure trust. The pure trust which was created, The North American Land Company, is still in existence today.

Q: *Why do the knowledgable-wealthy utilize pure trust organizations instead of wills, living trusts, and corporations?*

A: There are a number of reasons:

1. Because PTO's eliminate the estate shrinkage that is caused by probate costs and estate taxes. Wills are created in the expectation of death. Pure Trusts are created in the expectation of life. A pure trust creator, beneficiary, or trustee may die, but a PTO does not die unless its trustees dissolve it.

"A trust for probate avoidance is a lawful, irrevocable separate legal entitle," — *Harwood v. Tracy, 118 Mo. 631, 24 SW 214.*

2. Because PTO's maintain complete personal and financial privacy. PTO documents and bank statements are not subject to IRS audit or other government subpoenas.

"The trustees of a trust have all the power necessary to carry out the obligations which they assume. Their books and records are not subject to review or subpoenas." — *Smith v. Morse, Ca 524.*

"Concerning privacy, a trust organization created under the United States Constitution's 'Right of Contract' cannot be abridged." — *Waterman v. Mackenzie, 138 US 252 (1981).*

"A pure trust is established by contract, and any law or procedure in its operation, denying or obstructing contract rights, impairs contract obligation and is, therefore, in violation of the United States Constitution." — *Burnett v. Smith, 240 SW 1007 (1822) US Supreme Court.*

3. Because PTO's limit personal and business liability. If what you personally own at present is placed into a PTO, you will no longer "own it". If you are sued (and you lose), a judgment may only go against you and what you personally own. It cannot attach itself to a PTO, which is a separate legal entity.

"[Pure] Trust property cannot be held under attachment nor sold upon execution for the trustee's personal debts." — *Clew v. Jamison, 182 US 461, 21 S Ct 645.*

4. Because PTO's, as we have said, have no tax requirements.

"A pure trust is not illegal if formed for the express purpose of avoiding taxation." — *Edward v. Commissioner, 415 Fd2 578,582 (10th Cir. 1969); Weeks v. Sibly, (DC), 269 F 155.*

"The legal right of a taxpayer to decrease the amount of what otherwise would be his taxes, or altogether avoid them, by means which the law permits, cannot be doubted." — *Justice George Sutherland, Gregory v. Helvering, 239 US 465, 469 (1934).*

"As to the astuteness of taxpayers in ordering their affairs so as to minimize taxes, we have said that, 'The meaning of a line in the law is that you intentionally may go as close to it as you can if you do not pass it'." — *Superior Oil Co. v. Mississippi, 280 US 390, 395-96.*

"All subjects over which the sovereign power of the state extends [i.e., corporations or other statutory entities] are objects of taxation [and regulation], but those over which it does not extend are exempt from taxation [and exempt from regulation]. This proposition may almost be pronounced as self-evident. The sovereignty of the state extends to everything which exists by its authority or its permission. — *McCulloch v. Maryland, 4 Wheat, 316.*

"The Pure Trust derives no power, benefit, or privilege from any statute." — *Crocker v. Malley, 264 US 144; Gleason v. McKay, 134 Mass 419; Goldwater v. Oltman, 292 P 624 (1920).*

5. Because PTO's can engage in any lawful enterprise or activity.

"It has been held that public policy is not offended by permitting a business to be carried on by trustees who limit their liability to the trust estate...[N]or do statutes authorizing limited liability partnerships and corporations by implication prohibit the creation of other types of organizations such a Business Trusts, enjoying similar immunity by virtue of the common law." — *14 Am Jur 2d, 58 ALR 462.*

6. Because PTO's may receive nominal income from any agents-trustees who have an employment contract with the PTO, this employment contract may provide that all income received from a firm, company, or individual for which or whom services have been rendered must be released to the PTO. Therefore, no government agency has the right to take income earned by the PTO in this manner, add it to the income of the trustee(s), and then force the trustee(s) to pay income taxes on it.

"The Internal Revenue Service has recognized that amounts received by an Agent on behalf of a Principal and turned over to the Principal are not taxable to the Agent under Sec. 61(A) of the code." — *Internal Revenue Ruling, 76-479.*

The United States Supreme court [Lucas v. Earl, 281 UPS 111 (1930)] held that tax responsibility can be shifted when the "tree" (that which produced the income) and not just the "fruit" (the income itself) is conveyed. Moreover, under these circumstances, the third party employer cannot be held responsible for withholding income taxes. — *See IRS Regulations, Cec. 31-1401(d)1; Rev. Rul. 57-145, C.B. 1957-1, p. 332; and 13 Am Jur 2d (Business Trusts).*

7. Because, if the Trustee and-or spouse signs a contract with the PTO that requires he-she-them to live and work on the premises in order to perform all of the services required, then such premises shall be supplied and maintained, all utilities shall be paid, and transportation shall be provided at no cost to the Trustee(s), and the value of these items is not considered taxable income to the Trustee(s).

"By the common law, every Trustee has the duty of exercising reasonable care in the custody of the fiduciary estate, unless he is relieved of such duty by agreement, statute, or order of Court. — *U.S. ex rel Willoghby v. Howard, 302 US 445, 58 S CT 309, 82 EEd 352.*

"There shall be excluded from gross income of an employee, the value of any meals or lodging furnished to him by his employer, but only if: (a) In the case of meals, these are furnished on the business premises of the employer, or (b) In the case of lodging, the employee is required to accept such lodging on the business premises of his employer as a condition of employment." — *Internal Revenue Code, Sec. 119.*

8. Because PTO's have full sovereign rights guaranteed by the Constitution for the United States of America (1787) and its Articles in amendment. Corporations and other business entities do not have such rights.

"The fact that a business trust is not regarded as a legal entity distinct from its trustees, if a true trust...may result in this advantage to the trust, which a corporation does not possess; the trust consists of individuals...who are Citizens, and who, therefore, are entitled to certain rights and immunities such as those guaranteed by the privileges and immunities clause [Art. IV, Sect. 2, Cl. 1] of the Federal Constitution, which do not apply to corporations." — *Morrissey, et al., Trustees v. Commissioner,*

296 US 344, 80 L Ed 363, 56 S Ct 289, 156 ALR, p. 50, para. 3.

"The individual may stand upon his constitutional rights as a Citizen. He is entitled to carry on his private business in his own way. His power to contract is unlimited. He owes no duty to the State of to his neighbors to divulge his business or to open his doors to investigation... He owes no duty to the State, since he receives nothing therefrom, beyond the protection of his life and property. His rights are such as existed by the Law of the Land, long antecedent to the organization of the State, and can only be taken from him by due process of the law and in accordance with the Constitution. He owes nothing to the public so long as he does not trespass upon their rights." — *Hale v. Henkle, 201 US 43 at 74, (U.S. Supreme Court).* (Repeated on p.57).

"One of the objectives of business trust is to obtain for the trust associates most of the advantages of corporations without the authority of any legislative act and with the freedom from the restrictions and regulations generally imposed by law upon corporations." — *13 Am Jur 2d, p. 379, Para. 51.*

"A trust relationship comes under the realm of equity, based upon the common law, and is not subject to legislative restrictions, as are corporations and other organizations created by legislative authority. — *Elliot v. Freeman, 20 U.S. 178.*

9. Because assets may be transferred into the PTO (and thereby protected, presented, improved upon, and held for the present and future benefit of self and family) without negative tax consequences.

Market Value, for the purpose of the internal revenue law, is the price at which a seller is willing to sell at a fair price and a buyer willing to buy at a fair price, both having reasonable knowledge of the facts in the trade. On the creator's side, the trust certificates received have no reportable or determinable value to be declared. The trust organization receives property at its current market value. If the same property is later sold, only the amount beyond the creator's basis is recognized as taxable, as the appreciated value is part of the trusts assets. The property recognizes that a taxable status exists when transferred into the trust organization, but any tax payment is deferred until distributed from the trust organization to the beneficiaries." — *American National Bank of St. Joseph v. U.S., 92 F Supp 403 (1950).*

"[No] tax is assessed on the conveyance of property to a Trust because it constitutes a tax-free trade and exchange for Trust Certificates which have only a contingent future interest of indeterminable value. The tax is not evaded or avoided. It is merely deferred." — *Brunet v. Logan, 283 US 404.*

Q: *In the case above, the court ruled that, "The tax is not evaded or avoided. It is merely deferred." Does this me an that taxes are due and payable when a PTO is terminated?*

A: The IRS sees taxes as due and payable every time a taxpaying entity receives "income". But what if another PTO receives the final distribution? According to Diane H. Whitby, Chief, Accounting Branch, Internal

Revenue Service, Philadelphia, Pennsylvania, a PTO has no tax requirements. Therefore, no taxable event with a taxpaying entity has occurred.

Q: *Could a PTO be set up to cover profits that have been made in the past?*

A: **No.** A PTO can greatly reduce or eliminate federal income taxes, self-employment taxes, estate taxes, and probate costs, but it can only do so starting from the date of its creation. To attempt to back-date a PTO would put benefits to be derived from it in the future at risk.

Q: *Can a PTO claim a refund for taxes paid in the past?*

A: Only entities that have paid taxes can go back in time to claim a refund. Since a PTO doesn't have any tax requirements, it cannot claim your refund or anyone else's. If a refund is due you, you will have to claim it for yourself, using your name and your taxpayer identification number and not those of the PTO.

Q: *How are assets such as cars and boats transferred into a PTO?*

A: Sometimes it is best to leave assets such as cars and boats titled in the name of an individual but to exchange all of the equity with the PTO and have the PTO record a corresponding security interest in the assets using a demand note and UCC 1. (The interest would have to be satisfied and released by the PTO before the title could be transferred to anyone else, though.) This would protect the individual in terms of liability because, if an individual has no equity in a property, no equities can be seized from or taken by way of judgment against the individual.

Q: *If the legality of my PTO is challenged, who can I talk to?*

A: Although no instance in the past is known where the validity of a PTO has been challenged in court by the IRS, there are several persons who offer assistance in the realm of PTO's and your common law rights. There are both "non-lawyers" (persons who have graduated from law school but who do not wish to join a bar association) and lawyers. Most of these individuals work on a consulting basis with hourly rates of $150 dollars or less.

Because its previous attacks were not successful, the IRS does not like to acknowledge the existence of PTO's.

It seems like the IRS is making an effort to "keep a lid on" the spread of PTO's. The tactic of the IRS is not to attack the PTO entity, but to attack the people who promote them. These attacks range from "bad-mouthing" to setting up elaborate "sting" operations in which the trust promoter has allegedly become involved in money laundering.

Because of these IRS tactics, most lawyers will not consult with any individual who will not sign a statement certifying that he-she is not a government agent and that the assets and-or income involved have not resulted from illegal activities.

Q: *where can I look for additional information about PTO's?*

A: Volume 13 of American Jurisprudence (2nd Edition, 1985) examines court rulings that concern a variety of forms of trust organizations. PTO's have some of the qualities of the trust organizations that are described in this legal reference work as Common Law Trusts, Business Trusts, and Massachusetts Business Trusts. In addition, you may study *Income Taxation of Trusts, Estates, Grantors, and Beneficiaries* by Jeffrey N. Pennell (West Publishing Company), or *The Federal Tax Guide* (Legal Forms 2d.)

Q: *How does a Pure Trust Organization work for the Founder of a Fraternal Association?*

A: **Step 1:** The **Founder/Trustor** of a desired PTO contracts with a **Creator/Protector** for an exchange of the **Founder/Trustor's property** in return for the right to the final disposition of assets when and if the PTO is ever dissolved. This contract involves a *quid pro quo* (equal value for equal value) exchange, i.e. real property for the right to any residual assets of the PTO upon dissolution.

Step 2: Through the process of the Exchange, the **Creator/Protector** assigns the **Founder/Trustor's property** to a legal entity called a PTO. In the exchange, the **Founder/Trustor** offers and receives $25 dollars of silver in consideration for 100% of the right to the final distribution of the assets of the PTO whenever and if ever it is dissolved.

Step 3: The **Creator/Protector** will then appoint and employ the **Founder/Trustor** to be the **Managing/Trustee** of a majority/unrelated **Board of Trustees** who will administer and direct the affairs of the PTO according to the terms of the PTO.

Step 4: The **Founder/Trustor** designates the Beneficiaries of the trust.

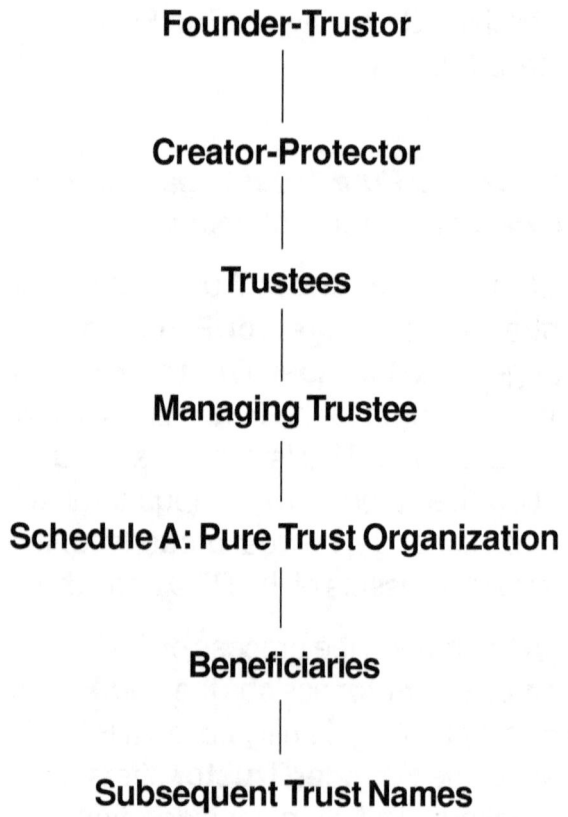

Founder-Trustor

Creator-Protector

Trustees

Managing Trustee

Schedule A: Pure Trust Organization

Beneficiaries

Subsequent Trust Names

7

Common Law Jurisdiction vs. Statutory Law Jurisdiction

Very few U.S. citizens know that they have a fundamental choice: To live their lives and conduct their businesses under common law jurisdiction or statutory law jurisdiction. Common Law is the law of the land, the law of the Constitution. Statutory law is the laws of the federal government and the several state municipalities thereof.

The U.S. Constitution is a Common-Law Statement. In the United States, Common Law is the law of the land.

• "It [The Constitution] must be interpreted in the light of Common Law, the principles and history of which were familiarly known to the framers of the Constitution. The language of the Constitution could not be understood without reference to the Common Law." — *U.S. v. Wong Kin Ark, 169 U.S. 649, 18 S. Ct. 456.*

• "Law of the Land" means "The Common Law," — *Taylor v. Porter, 4 Hill. 140, 146 (1843) - Justice Bronson; and State v. Simon, 2 Spears 761, 767 (1884) - Justice O'Neal.*

• "The U.S. adopted the Common Laws of England with the Constitution. — *Coldwell v. Hiss, 176 S.E. 383 (1934).*

7

- "The United States is entirely a creature of the Federal Constitution, its power and authority has no other source, and it can only act in accordance with all the limitations imposed by the Constitution." — *Reid v. Covert, 354 U.S. 1, 1 L. Ed. 2nd. 1148 (1957).*

- "The rights and liberties of the citizens of the United States are not protected by custom and tradition alone, they are preserved from the encroachments of government by express/enumerated provisions of the Federal Constitution." — *Reid v. Covert, 354 U.S. 1, 1 L. Ed. 2nd. 1148 (1957).*

- "The prohibitions of the Federal Constitution are designed to apply to all branches of the national government and cannot be nullified by the executive or by the executive and the senate combined." — Reid v. Covert, 354 U.S. 1, 1 L. Ed. 2nd. 1148 (1957).

- "Where rights as secured by the Constitution are involved, there can be no rule making or legislation which will abrogate them." — *Miranda v. Ariz., 384 U.S. 436 at 491 (1966).*

- "Congress may not, by any definition it may adopt, conclude the matter, since it cannot by legislation alter the Constitution." — *Eisner v. McComber, 252 U.S. 189 at 207. The IRS makes this distinction between the two kinds of law:*
  1. Common law comprises the body of principles and rules of action relating to government and security of persons and property which derive their authority solely from usages and custom or from judgments and decrees

of courts recognizing, affirming, and enforcing such usages and customs.

2. Statutory law refers to laws enacted and established by a legislative body."— *IRS Manual, page 5041.1 Section 222.1.*

Much of the original U.S. common law has been codified in a single Federal statute, called the Uniform Commercial Code. The UCC provides the mechanism for making the choice between common law jurisdiction and statutory jurisdiction. It also states that the failure to make the choice results in the loss of common law rights.

"When a waivable right or claim is involved, the failure to make a reservation thereof, causes a loss of the right, and bars its assertion at a later day." — *UCC 1-207.4.*

The specific method for reserving your common-law rights – for choosing to operate under common law jurisdiction — is to write below your signature "Without Prejudice UCC 1-207 (changed to 1-308)." You could use this phrase on your driver's license, on bank signature cards, on checks, and on contracts.

Case Law on Jurisdiction

• "The law provides that once State and Federal Jurisdiction has been challenged, it must be proven." — *Main v. Thiboutot, 100 S. Ct. 2502 (1980).*

• "Jurisdiction can be challenged at any time." — *Basso v. Utah Power & Light Co., 495 F 2nd 906 at 910.*

• "Where there is absence of proof of jurisdiction, all administrative and judicial proceedings are a nullity, and confer no right, offer no protection, and afford no justification, and may be rejected upon direct collateral attack." — *Thompson v. Tolmie, 2 Pet. 157, 7 L. Ed. 381; and Griffith v. Frazier, 8 Cr. 9, 3 L. Ed. 471.*

WHAT MAKES THE PURE CONTRACT TRUST SUCH A POWERFUL INSTRUMENT?

The Pure Contract-Trust is a Common-Law "Identity" ("legal person"), based on the unlimited right to contract, and not subject to statutory jurisdiction

• "No State shall... pass any bill... or law impairing the obligation of contracts..." — *U.S. Constitution, Article I, Section 10 (1787).*

• A trust is a legal entity. — *Burnett v. Smith, 240 S.E. 1007 (1822).*

• A Pure Trust is a contractual relationship in Trust form. — *Berry v. McCourt, 204 N.E. 2nd 235 (1965).*

• A Trust organization created under the U.S. constitutional right of contract cannot be abridged. The agreement, when executed, creates a Federal organization not under the laws passed by any of the several (State) legislatures. — *Crocker v. MacCloy, 649 U.S. Sup. 39 at 270.*

• A Pure Contract Trust is not subject to legislative control. The U.S. Supreme Court holds that Trust relationship comes under the realm of equity, based upon the common law, and is not subject to legislative restrictions as are corporations and other organizations created by legislative authority. — *Elliot v. Freeman, 220 U.S. 178 (1911).*

The Pure Contract-Trust is a Contractual Agreement guaranteed by the US Constitution.

• A Pure Trust is established by contract, and any law or procedure in its operation, denying or obstructing contract rights, impairs contract obligation and is therefore violative of the U.S. Constitution. — *Burnett v. Smith, 240 S.W. 1007 (1922).*

• The creator of a Pure Trust may mold and give it any shape he chooses, and he or the trustees may provide for the appointment of a successor or successors to the trustee or trustees, upon such terms as he may choose to impose. "It is established by legal precedent that pure trusts are lawful, valid business organizations." — *Shaw v. Paine, 12 Allen (Mass) 293; and Harwood v. Tracy, 118 MO. 631, 24 SW 214.*

The Pure Contract Trust can engage in any lawful business in any State, and anywhere in the world.

• "It is established by legal precedent that pure trusts are lawful, valid business organizations." — *Baker v. Stern, 216 NW 147, 58 A.L.R. 642.*

• A trust created and recorded in one state is valid in all states. — *Newhall v. McGill, 212 P 2nd 764.*

• The Trust is not limited to any given state in conducting business. — *Shirk v. Lafayette, 52 F 957.*

• The Pure Trust can engage in any kind of lawful business that individuals, partnerships, or corporations might engage in, as evident from the wide variety of business pursuits for which Pure Trusts have been organized: Operating and management of apartment houses — Helvering v. Coleman-Gilbert Assn., 296 U.S. 369; Oil well development — Helvering v. Cones, 296 U.S. 375; Real estate business — Crocker v. Malley, 249 U.S. 23; Purchasing, improving, holding and selling land and buildings and operating an office building — Elliot v. Freeman, 220 U.S. 178 (1911); Production of motion pictures — Goldwater v. Oltman, 210 Cal 408; building and equipping racing speedway — *Chas. Nelson Co. v. Morton, 106 Cal. App. 144; Real estate business — Schumann-Heink v. Folsom 328 Ill., 321.*

The Pure Contract Trust may reduce its tax liability

• "A pure trust is not illegal if formed for the express purpose of avoiding taxation." — *Weeks v. Sibley, (D.C.) 269 F 155.*

• "Dignity of contract cannot be set aside because a tax benefit results either by design or accident." — *Edwards v. Commissioner, 415 F 2nd 578, 582, 10th Cir. (1969).*

• "Anyone may arrange his affairs so that his taxes shall be as low as possible. He is not bound to choose that pattern which best pays the Treasury. There is not even a patriotic duty to increase one's taxes. Over and over again courts have said that there is nothing sinister in so arranging affairs as to keep taxes as low as possible, everyone does it, rich and poor alike and all do right, for nobody owes any public duty to pay more than the law demands." — *Helvering v. Gregory, 60 Federal (2nd) 809. Judge learned Hand.*

(Note: Certain trusts are taxed as associations. However, there is sound legal evidence that the Pure Contract Trust is not an association.) "We perceive no ground for grouping the two — beneficiaries and trustees — together, in order to turn them into an association, by uniting their contrasted functions and powers, although they are in no proper sense associated." — *Hecht v. Malley, 265 U.S. 144.*

• If property received in exchange has no fair market value, it does not represent taxable gain to the recipient. — *Burnet v. Logan, 283 U.S. 404.*

• Subscription to stock in Common Law Trust was held not a gift but an investment. — *Palmer et. al. v. Taylor et. al., 269 S.W. 996 (1925).*

• Gift tax applies only to transfers by gift with less than full and adequate consideration. — *Tyson v. Commissioner, 146 F 2nd. 50 (1944).*

The Pure Contract Trust may remunerate directors or other individuals, who may pay taxes on such remuneration

• "The right to labor and to its protection from unlawful interference is a Constitutional as well as a Common Law right. Every man has a natural right to the fruits of his own industry." — *48 Am. Jur. 2nd., Section 2 at Pg. 80.*

• "A State may not impose a charge for the enjoyment of a right secured by the Federal Constitution." — *Murdock v. Pennsy, 319 U.S. 105.*

• "Where rights secured by the Constitution are involved, there can be no rule making or legislation which would abrogate them." — *Miranda v. Ariz., 384 U.S. 436 at 491 (1966).*

• "The cooperative taxpayer fares much worse than the individual who relies upon his constitutional rights. Only the rare taxpayer would be likely to know that he could refuse to produce his records to Internal Revenue Service Agents." — *U.S. v. Dickerson, 413 F 2d 1116.*

• "In numerous cases where the IRS has sought enforcement of its summons pursuant to statute (26 U.S.C. 7402), courts have held that a taxpayer may refuse production of personal books, and records by assertion of his privilege against self-incrimination." — *Hill v. Philpott, 445 F 2d 144; and Stuart v. U.S. 416 F 2d 459; and U.S. v. Kleckner, 273 F Supp 251.*

• Treasury Department regulations, construing laws relating to taxation, are not conclusive. Doubts in taxation statutes are resolved in favor of taxpayer. — *Hell Mich. v. Hell man, 18 F 2D 239 (1927).*

The Pure Contract Trust is not subject to probate or estate taxes

• A Trust, for probate avoidance, is a lawful, irrevocable, separate entity. — *Shaw v. Paine, 12 Allen (Mass) 293; and Harwood v. Tracy, 118 Mo. 631, 24 S.W. 214.*

(Note: Although the Pure Contract Trust has a termination date, it can be renewed and need not be subject to "death". The first trust similar to the Pure Contract Trust on record in the U.S. was drawn up by Patrick Henry in 1765. Called the North American Land Company, it is believed to be still in operation at the time of writing.)

• Succeeding trustees take title to the property subject to the same conditions as in the hands of the original trustees. — *Bisbee v. McKay, 102 N.E. 327.*

• Federal estate tax is an excise on transfer of interests in property that occurs as a result of death. — *Old Kent Bank & Trust Co. v. U.S., 349 F Supp. 792 (1972).*

The Pure Contract Trust has no reporting obligations to any government or state

• The Trustees of a Trust have all the powers necessary to carry out the obligations which they assume. Their books and records are not subject to review or subpoena. — *Smith v. Morse, 2 CA 524; Boyd v. U.S., 116 U.S. 618; Silverthorne Lumber Co. v. U.S., 241 U.S. 385.*

The Pure Contract Trust contains a clause forbidding the parties, including managing directors(s), to reveal confidential information about the trust without the unanimous decision of the trustees.

• The Court will support the trustees in carrying out the terms of their trust contract and agreement. — *Clew v. Jamison, 182 U.S. 461, 21 S. Ct. 645.*

• Concerning privacy, a trust organization created under the U.S. Constitutional right of contract cannot be abridged. The agreement, when executed, creates a federal organization not under the laws passed by any of the several [State and Congress] legislatures. — *U.S. v. Carruthers, 209 F2s 21 (1925); and Waterman v. MacKenzie, 138 US 252 (1981).*

The Pure Contract Trust has the constitutional protections of right to privacy, freedom from unwarranted search and seizure, to refrain from self-incrimination, and all other individual rights bestowed by the U.S. Constitution

• "There is a clear distinction in this particular case between an individual and a corporation, and that the latter has no right to refuse to submit its books and papers for an examination at the suit of the State. The individual may stand upon his constitutional rights as a citizen. He is entitled to carry on his private business in his own way. His power to contract is unlimited. He owes no such duty [to submit his books and papers for an examination] to the State, since he receives nothing therefrom, beyond the protection of his life and property. His rights are such as existed by the law of the land [Common Law] long antecedent to the organization of the State, and can only be taken from him by due process of law, and in accordance with the Constitution. Among his rights are a refusal to incriminate himself, and the immunity of himself and his property from arrest or seizure except under a warrant of the law. He owes nothing to the public so long as he does not trespass upon their rights." — *Hale v. Henkle, 201 U.S. 43 at 47 (1905); and Pinkerton v. Verberg, 78 Mich. 573, 584.* (Repeated from p.41).

The Pure Contract Trust provides limited liability protection

• Trust property cannot be held under attachment nor sold upon execution, for the trustees' personal debts. — *Clew v. Jamison, 182 U.S. 461, 21 S. Ct. 645.*

• Personal liability of a Trustee cannot be enforced against the trust property. — *Mayo v. Moritz, 24 N.E. 1083 (1980).*

• Trustees and beneficiaries cannot be held liable for debts incurred by the trust. — *Hussey V. Arnold, 70 N.E. 87 (1904).*

Asset Protection

DECLARATION OF TRUST

Asset Protection

Trust I.D. # _____   (
                                  (
Creation Date _____   (
                                  (
When recorded mail to: (
                                  (
(l) _____   (
_____   (
_____   (
_____   (
                                  (
(2)_____   (
_____   (
_____   (
_____   (
                                  (_____

DECLARATION OF TRUST

ARTICLE I

PARTIES TO THIS TRUST AGREEMENT:

Trustor/s:

(3) _____
_____
_____
_____

(4)_____
_____
_____
_____

Trustee/s:

(5) _____
_____
_____
_____

(6) _____
_____
_____
_____

BENEFICIARIES OF TRUST:

Beneficiary No. 1 _____

Beneficiary No. 2 _____

Beneficiary No. 3 _____

Beneficiary No. 4 _____

Beneficiary No. 5 _____

Names withheld in accordance with International Privacy Standards applicable, a separate file is held with the actual names of the Beneficiaries by the current Trustee in charge.

ARTICLE III

PURPOSE:

The Trustor transfers to the Trustee all property listed in Schedule A attached to this agreement for the uses and purpose specified in this agreement. Trustee shall hold, manage, invest and reinvest the property transferred and distribute receiving(s) and principal to the designated beneficiaries according to the terms and conditions of the trust or separate trusts established by the agreement. The good faith is further strengthened by the watchful eye of our God over the actions of all trustees involved now and in the future.

ARTICLE IV

NO POWERS RESERVED BY TRUSTOR

This trust is irrevocable. It is amendable only by the trustee/s and must be held and distributed according to its terms. Additional property may be added to this trust at any time by any person, which property shall be held by Trustee under the terms of this trust and the terms apply at the time of addition subject to future acceptance by Trustee.

ARTICLE V

POWERS OF THE TRUSTEE

(A) Trustees shall distribute the net receiving(s) to or for the benefit of the beneficiaries. All receiving(s), by and in any form, shall be deemed as currently distibutable.

(B) If, in the opinion of the Trustee, the beneficiaries are in need of additional receiving(s) to provide adequately for his, her or its health, education and support in reasonable comfort, Trustee shall forward, extract, and/or for the benefit of the beneficiaries forward such receiving(s) from the principal of the trust from time to time as it shall determine in its discretion to be necessary and/or appropriate for such purposes, by whatever means and creation necessary to ensure privacy and anonymity.

(C) On the death or the beneficiaries, Trustee shall forward the then remaining principal and undistrubuted receiving(s) to or among such person(s) or entities, to the beneficiaries' estate in such amounts or proportions and in such manner, including outright, or intrust, as the beneficiary(ies) shall appoint or in the alternative, trustee appoints, in his, her or it's Last Will if such makes specific reference to the exercise of this power.

(D) On the death of the beneficiary(ies), if or to the extent distribution is not made pursuant to exercise of the power of appointment granted in the previous paragraph, Trustee shall distribute the balance of principal and undistributed receiving(s) to the beneficiary(ies) surviving issue, such issue to take by right or representation.

(E) If, by the previous paragraph, any distribution is required to be made to a [minor] recipient, the receiving(s) so required to be distributed shall be indefeasibly vested in the [minor] until such time as the [minor] attains his or her majority or dies, whichever first occurs. Trustee may distribute so much of the receiving(s) and principal to or for the benefit of the [minor] recipient as in the Trustee's sole discretion is necessary to provide for his, her or it's health, education and support in reasonable comfort. Any receiving(s) not distributed may be added to the principal of such receivings and tangibly invested as a part thereof. Then when the minor attains his, her or it's majority or dies, which ever first occurs, the then remaining principal and undistributed receiving(s) shall be distributed to him, her or it, if living, or to his, her or it's estate, if deceased.

(F) If, or to the extent, the above provisions do not provide for distribution of the trust estate, or any part thereof, such interest shall be distributed free of trust upon termination of all prior estates or interest to the intestate heirs of the beneficiary(ies) as then determined by the laws of the established choice of original jurisdiction law, as then in affect, in accord with this document.

(G) No Trustee or successor Trustee shall be required to give any bond or other security.

(H) The trustee if deemed necessary and appropriate, may move the trust situs to any state or nation pursuant to choice of law. I accord with same this trust's choice of law is deemed within International Law located at The Hague in the Netherlands, at this juncture.

ARTICLE VI

DISTRIBUTION QUALIFICATION

(A) Trustee is not to recognize any transfer, mortgage, pledge, hypothecation, assignment or order of a beneficiary(ies) which anticipates the payment of any part of the receivings or principal. The receivings and principal of the trust estate shall not be subject to attachments, garnishments, creditor's bills or executions to satisfy any debts, obligations or torts of any bankruptcy proceedings initiated by or against any beneficiary(ies).

(B) Required distributions of receivings to a beneficiary(ies) shall be deemed as currently distributable and in the sole discretion of the trustee.

Distributions of receivings or principal to any beneficiary(ies) may be:

1. Paid directly to the beneficiary(ies); or

2. Deposited in any bank to the credit of the beneficiary(ies) in an account carried in the beneficiary(ies)'s name either alone or jointly with others; or

3. Expended for the benefit of the beneficiary(ies); or

4. Paid to someone who has undertaken the responsibility lawful or voluntarily, for the support and maintenance of the beneficiary(ies); or

5. Reinvested and maintained within this trust or another trust for the benefit of the beneficiary(ies).

After making any payment or distribution, trustee shall be fully discharged of liability with respect to and further accountability for such payment or distribution.

(C) If the market value of the aggregate assets in the principal account totals less than the accrual value of fifty one ounce (99.9%) Gold coins, this trust may be terminated in the sole discretion of the Trustee and distributed to the beneficiaries in proportion to their receivings interests; or, if such interests are indefinite, then to the receivings, beneficiaries in such equitable proportions, Trustee shall determine quantity distributable.

(D) Trustee is directed to regard the receivings of beneficiaries at any given time as having primary rights under this agreement and Trustee is directed to consider only the welfare of receivings to beneficiaries in the exercise of discretionary powers and disregard the receivings of any successor beneficiaries. Any discretionary right to use principal shall include the right to exhaust principal for such purpose. No beneficiary(ies) shall have any right to compel Trustee to make any discretionary payment or expenditure of receivings or question the propriety of any discretionary payment or expenditure of receivings made by Trustees. Any discretionary determination made by Trustee shall be final as to all beneficiaries.

(E) On the death of a beneficiary entitled to receiving distributions, any accrued or undistributed receivings shall continue to be treated as receivings and shall be held and accounted for, or distributed, in the same manner as if the receivings had been received and accrued after the beneficiary(ies)'s death.

F) Trustee's discretion to distribute principal to or for the benefit of a beneficiary(ies) shall include authority to pay expenses of last illness, funeral and burial expenses of the beneficiary(ies), after death; provided that any calculations of successor interests shall be made as if any such payments had been made from the principal prior to the death of such beneficiary(ies).

(G) If any trust created by this agreement is still in existence twenty-one (21) years after the death of all persons listed in Article II and their descendants who are living on the date of this trust, all shares shall immediately vest in the persons then entitled to the receivings and in proportion to their receivings interest or, if such interest are indefinite, then to the receivings and in proportion to their receivings interests or, if such interest is indefinite, then to the receivings beneficiaries in such equitable proportions as Trustee shall determine.

ARTICLE VII

POWERS AND DUTIES OF TRUSTEE

(A) With respect to this trust and any sub-trusts created by this agreement, and property thereof, Trustee shall have all powers given it by law and all powers which may be exercised by individuals owning similar property in their own rights. Without restricting the generality of the foregoing, the following powers are set forth by way of illustration of the extent of powers granted and not by way of limitation, to be exercised from time to time by Trustee in its discretion.

1. To receive additions to any trusts established under this agreement from any source and to administer such additions (receivings) according to the terms of this agreement;

2. To retain indefinitely without liability for loss, any property or

receivings in property received in kind by Trustee as an addition to the trust estate regardless of degree of risk affect on diversification or non-productivity of the asset;

3. To sell, exchange, lease, grant options to purchase and execute contracts concerning trust property for such considerations and upon such conditions and payment terms as Trustee may determine without regard to the termination date of any trust;

4. To invest and reinvest trust receivings from time to time in bonds, notes, debentures, corporate stocks of any class, trust interests including common trust funds and investment trust shares, real estate or any other kind or real and personal property or business interest without being limited by any statute or rule of law concerning proper investments for Trustee, to assign undivided interests in investments to any separate trust or shares established by this agreement;

5. To participate in the management of business enterprises, as stockholder, partner or principal, to participate in any organization or reorganization of a business enterprise committing and transferring trust assets or funds for such purpose; to vote stock by proxy or otherwise; to deposit or transfer securities to protective or voting committees or similar bodies; and to exercise any options, execute any documents and delegate authority to act in its behalf in futherance of any of these activities;

6. To operate, improve or develop real estate; to construct, alter, raze, or repair buildings or structures on real estate; to partition, subdivide, dedicate to public use, grant easements or other rights with respect to or otherwise deal with real estate;

7. To employ and compensate attorneys, assistants of counsel, accountants, brokers, agents and custodians;

8. To pay all costs and expenses of the trust and its property, including reasonable compensation to Trustee for its services not to exceed one silver dollar piece per year plus expenses necessary to conduct the business of the trust.;

9. To arbitrate, settle, compromise, contest, foreclose, extend or abandon claims or demands in favor of or against the trust property my mortgage or pledge;

10. To borrow at interest money from any banking institution or from any other sources and to assume indebtedness and encumber trust property by mortgage or pledge;

11. To allocate receipts and disbursements between principal and receivings on a reasonable basis giving consideration to its usual custom and the lawful as exchange and excise of which may be in effect from time to time in making its determinations; to establish reserves out of receivings, if it sees fir, for depreciation of property, and anticipated expenses;

12. To enter into any transaction authorized by this article with Trustees or personal representatives of other trusts or estates in which any beneficiary(ies) of this trust agreement has an interest or which by its terms distributes to any trustee or trust established by this agreement, even though Trustee also serves the other trust or estate in a fiduciary capacity; and in such transaction to purchase property, or make loans on notes secured by property, even though similar or identical property constitutes a large proportion of the balance of the trust estate, and to retain any such property or note as if they had been received in kind as an addition to the trust estate.

13. To purchase and own policies of life insurance on the life of any beneficiary(ies) under this trust agreement; to pay premiums or charges on life insurance from income or principal; and to exercise any and all settlement options, right or incidents of ownership trustee may have over policies of life insurance; to purchase and own policies of life insurance on the life of the original trustor provided that the beneficiary(ies) of said life insurance is the trustors herein named.

14. To determine the market value of any investment for any purpose on the basis of such quotations or information as trustee deems pertinent and reliable;

15. To make any distribution or divisions of the trust property in cash or in kind of any currency, or both, and to allocate or alloy specific asset amounts to beneficiaries on the basis of current value determined by Trustee.

16. To contract, on behalf of the trust, with any company, corporation, or individual for services by either the company, corporation, or individual or by the trustee or any designated agent.

17. To collect, in the name of the trust, or if necessary in the name of the trustee or designated agent, any and all currency or property in kind due as the result of services or exchange by any agent acting in behalf of or in cooperation with said trust. If any currency(s) so collected are required to be collected in the name of the trustee or agent, the trust, through its trustee or beneficiaries, shall immediately have a lien under the claim of Right to any and all such currencies, receivings or property collected.

18. The trustee is hereby authorized to buy, sell, trade exchange and deal in stocks, bonds, securities and commodities of every nature, on margin or otherwise, and to engage in covered option writing, and in connection therewith to borrow currencies and to pledge any and all stocks, bonds, securities and commodities, and to execute any and all agreements on behalf of the trust which may be required to establish said margin accounts.

(A) No person dealing with, making payments to or delivering property to trustee shall be obliged to inquire as to the powers of the trustee nor to see the application of any currencies, receiving or property delivered to trustee.

(B) Until trustee shall have written notice of any event or the existence of any document upon which the right to payments under this agreement may depend, trustee shall incur no liability for disbursements made in good faith to persons whose interest may have been affected by the event or by the existence of such document.

(C) A trustee may at any time by giving thirty (30) days written notice to each adult beneficiary(ies) then entitled to receive income from the trust, resign. On such resignation, a successor trustee shall be selected by the resigning trustee. If selection of a successor trustee has not been made by the effective date of a resignation, the resigning trustee or any adult beneficiary(ies) may petition for the appointment of a trustee in any appropriate venue decided within.

(D) A trustee may at any time and from time to time petition any appropriate court to have trust accounting judicially settled.

(E) In the event of the death of the trustee, a successor trustee shall be selected by a separate authorization made by the trustee prior to his death. In the event that a successor trustee has not been made or is unwilling to accept, any adult beneficiary(ies) may petition for the appointment of a trustee in any appropriate court.

(F) In the event the trustee becomes incapacitated or temporarily leaves the jurisdiction of the trust, trustee may delegate his duties, authority and/or responsibilities to any person he so designates. Such designation shall be written and shall be effective only in the absence of this agreement.

(G) Trustee may not divulge or reveal the names of the beneficiary(ies) and/or other terms of private contract between trustor and trustee. Trust agreement shall be used for confidential creation of account(s) with a selected bank under confidentiality provisions only.

ARTICLE VIII

INTERPRETATIONS

(A) No significance is to be attached to the use of singular or plural designations or the uses of the masculine, feminine, or neuter gender in this agreement. Each designation or gender shall be construed to include the others where appropriate.

(B) The usage of the word "receivings" shall include any property of any kind donated by any being, trust or entity, not to exclude currency property of others.

(C) This trust agreement shall be construed and regulated within International Law Located at the Hague in the Netherlands as host state.

SCHEDULE A

1. Established Donated amount of Lawful Currency:

____ 25 dollars in Silver Coin _____

_____

_____

2. Land and Private Property described as follows:

_____
_____
_____

3. Modes of Travel and Conveyance as follows:

_____
_____
_____

4. Insurance Policies and Types as follows:

_____
_____
_____

5. Other:

_____
_____
_____
_____
_____
_____
_____
_____
_____
_____
_____

IN WITNESS WHEREOF, Trustor has hereunto signed this trust and trustee has caused its name to be subscribed by its duly authorized agent:

_____
Trustee

_____
Trustee

_____
Trustor

_____
Trustor

STATE OF _____)
) SS.
County of _____)

On the _____ day of _____, _____,

before me _____ the undersigned, a Notary Public,

personally appeared _____

known to me (or satisfactorily proven) to be the person(s) whose

names(s) is/are subscribed to the above instrument and acknowledged

that _____ he _____ executed the same for the

purposes therein contained.

IN WITNESS WHEREOF, I hereunto set my hand and official seal.

                                    _____
                                                Notary Public

                                    My commission expires:

                                    _____

OTHER DOCUMENTS

Asset Protection

BILL OF SALE

I _____ residing at

_____ City _____

State _____, In consideration of _____

_____ paid to me by/from _____

_____ which is acknowledged, grant,

sell, transfer and deliver to _____

_____ the below listed property.

_____

_____

_____

_____

_____

And I, _____ for myself, my heirs, executors

and administrators, covenant and agree as follows:

1. I am the lawful owner of said property.
2. The property is/is not encumbered by lien holder.
3. I have good right to sell same.

Dated ———— ——, at _____

In the presence of: _____
                                        Witness

                       _____
                                        Witness

                       _____
                                        Witness

Asset Protection

AFFIDAVIT

When recorded mail to:

(1) _____

_____

_____

KNOW ALL MEN BY THESE PRESENTS:

That (2) _____

is/are the Trustee(s) and/or Designated agent(s) of the

(3) _____ created under the

U.S. Constitution Common Law — Right to Contract.

He/She is/are fully authorized to sign and cash checks, sell and buy, or otherwise exchange property.

He/She has/have full power and authority to do and perform all and every act and think whatsoever requisite and necessary to be done in the name of and on behalf of said trust.

IN WITNESS WHEREOF, I have hereunto set my hand,

on this the _____ day of _____, _____.

(4) _____

_____

(5) SUBSCRIBED AND SWORN to before me this _____
day of _____, _____.

_____
Notary Public
My Commission Expires:

_____

SUCCESSOR DESIGNATION

In the event of my, our passing-on or total incapacity, I, we

(1) _____ hereby appoint

(2) _____ to be successor

_____

Trustee(s) to the (3) _____

The successor Trustee or Trustees are to serve without bond and to have all powers granted by the said trust as if they were the original Trustee.

(4) _____

_____

(5) SUBSCRIBED AND SWORN to before me this _____ day of _____, _____.

_____
Notary Public

My Commission Expires:

_____

Asset Protection

QUIT-CLAIM DEED

SAMPLE FORMS CAN BE PURCHASED AT ANY
STATIONERY STORE WHICH SELLS LEGAL FORMS

CHANGES IN OWNERSHIP MUST BE FILLED IN BY
SELLERS AND DELIVERED TO PURCHASER OR
TRANSFEREE AT TIMES OF DELIVERY.

SUMMARY

1. Pure Trust Organizations are sovereign entities.

2. A Pure Trust has no tax requirements.

3. A Pure Trust has no need for an EIN or SSN.

4. Name your business as you would name a sole proprietorship.

5. Move all major assets out of your name.

6. The first Operating Entity should hold beneficial interest in all subsequent trusts.

7. A Family Trust can use your last name before the word Trust, i.e., "Smith Trust"", etc.

8. One individual cannot be both a Trustee and a Beneficiary. This separation makes the Trust Pure.

9. The Protector can terminate or appoint Trustees.

10. Trustees hold title to the property for the benefit of the Beneficiaries.

11. Trustees receive contractually agreed upon compensation for services rendered.

12. You can have one or many Trustees.

13. You can have one or many Trusts

14. A Trustee has no interest in the property.

15. If a relative(s) is a Beneficiary, you must have at least three unrelated Trustees in your Trust.

16. Trustees manage the Trust.

17. The Managing Trustee is an employee.

18. The Manager's name is shown in the minutes of the private Trust, only.

19. Beneficiaries have the right to the "beneficial interest" which is a right to the income, profits, proceeds, and use of the property.

20. The Trustee assigns to the Exchanger (Settlor) capital units (100%) in exchange for the property conveyed to the Trust, plus $25 in silver as valuable consideration.

21. Like any other private checking account, a Pure Trust is untainted by outside interests.

22. The Exchanger can keep or divide the capital unit as he sees fit.

23. You are the Exchanger; you contract with the Creator via an exchange; you donate an asset(s) in exchange for 25 dollars of silver received in hand, plus 100% of the final remaining assets when and if the Trust Is dissolved.

24. The Creator appoints the Fiduciary Owner (which is not you) to administer the Trust; the Fiduciary Owner then appoints you as Managing Director.

25. Money Orders & Promissory Notes are legal tender.

Asset Protection

"Take heed that ye do not your alms before men, to be seen of them : otherwise ye have no reward of your Father which is in heaven.

"Therefore when thou doest thine alms, do not sound a trumpet before thee, as the hypocrites do in the synagogues and in the streets, that they may have glory of men. Verily I say unto you, They have their reward.

"But when thou doest alms, let not thy left hand know what thy right hand doeth :

"That thine alms may be in secret : and thy Father which seeth in secret himself shall reward the openly."

— Matthew 6:1-4.

Asset Protection

Appendix

Asset Protection

Terminate Unsecured Debt

Unsecured debts can be purged using the **Fair Debt Collection Practices Act**. Credit history can be restored by using the **Fair Credit Reporting Act**.

You can defend yourself against Creditors with an understanding of contract law, Generally Accepted Accounting Principles, the rules of court,on the basis that banks do not loan anything.

Debt collectors can be defended against on the basis that an assignee cannot establish any contractual nexus to enforce a claim.

Banks are prohibited from loaning. They can't loan other depositor's money because of the *matching principle* under GAAP.

Banks can't loan out nor risk any of their own assets because of Federal Reserve regulations. *In order to accept a credit application or promissory note, the banks must convert the customer's note into a check and give it back to him.*

They can do this because banks have a monopoly on negotiable instruments. It is the customer who creates the currency, and funds the line of credit to himself. The customer is the depositor (the creditor). The banks conceal this fact by carrying out what appears to be a loan approval process for each customer. There is no loan from the bank.

One object of defending yourself against a creditor that has not assigned the account to a debt collector is to manipulate the creditor into a new agreement and/or force the account into collections.

The creditor can be sent a notice of final payment in expectation that the creditor will not dispute the payment or its terms in writing, thereby accepting it as payment in full. When the final payment is accepted, and the creditor has failed to respond or object to the notice of final payment, it makes it very difficult for them to maintain a claim against the account holder.

In practice, the creditor will call you to ask about late payments. It is prudent to take a record of the caller's name, company, mailing address, and phone and fax numbers, date and time of call, and then request that the caller limit communications with you only to writing. It is best to disconnect the call after obtaining this information and then to send a written correspondence making the same request.

If the calls continue, you can do this again or make a complaint with your state's attorney general's office. In most cases, the creditor will assign the account to collections. Once this happens, the third party collection efforts are regulated under the Fair Debt Collections Practices Act. The debt can be assigned, but that doesn't automatically mean that you have a contract with the new 3rd party debt collector; in fact you don't as long as you don't contract with them by acquiescence.

The third party assignee usually has no agreement with the debtor, so in order to recover the loss that it chose to incur; it needs the debtor's consent. This is usually obtained by deceit, by tricking the debtor into accepting a new obligation.

You can request from them a validation of the purported debt. This they're not going to be able to fully respond to – the collector never provided any services or products, neither is there an automatic obligation for you to pay. When the collector responds with anything but some written agreement, evidence of your consent or evidence of consideration (e.g. payment), they have failed to validate. Most collectors who receive this request will never pursue the collection. If the collector persists in ignoring your request for validation, a complaint to the Federal Trade Commission may be appropriate. Just listing the address for the FTC on the second notice is likely to get positive results.

Asset Protection

Responding to Offers or Demands

We have an unlimited ability to contract with our fellow human beings in any way that we choose. Our choices are dependent not upon our circumstances, but only upon our knowledge and will, and creative intelligence.

Whether in commerce or in law, or life, whenever someone demands something from us, it is an OFFER TO CONTRACT with that one.

There are only five ways we can respond to an offer to contract.

1) We can *ignore*;

2) We can *argue or contest*;

3) We can *reject or refuse it for cause without dishonor,* as long as it is an erroneous claim and no liability is in evidence (see UCC 3-501);

4) We can *accept*; or

5) We can *conditionally accept.*

Ignoring is dishonoring to the offerer and offeree. In commerce, ignoring means *agreement by acquiescence.* If someone sends us a bill and we ignore it, we have committed a commercial dishonor and have silently agreed that we owe it. The offeror becomes the creditor in the matter and we become the debtor/the slave.

Arguing is dishonoring to the offerer and offeree, as well — no matter how righteous the claim seems to be. Ultimately, no points of view are valid absolutely, and in a fight, force and deception are relied upon by all but the saintliest of parties. The debtor will certainly become the looser in the matter; the victor's creditorship may be a crime.

Honorably rejecting, and the **two ways of accepting,** are the only ways we can remain in honor, and take full responsibility for our life and our world, and not be a debtor/victim.

Full acceptance is appropriate when we agree with the substance and form of the offer.

Conditional acceptance is more appropriate when we are not certain and unsure about those things.

All conditional acceptances are counter-offers:

*"Sure, I'll go to town with you **if** you help me clean up that mess first"*.

OR *"Sure, I'll accept that **upon proof of your claim** in the form of an affidavit signed by you under penalties of perjury and under your unlimited, personal, commercial liability"*.

Learning how to **accept conditionally** is fundamental to learning how to remain a creditor and be able to freely control any situation.

Private vs. Public

It is important to know the difference between the private and the public, because we all have private and public identities.

We can handle private and public affairs from the private, but we cannot handle private affairs from the public. This latter is one of the biggest mistakes many people make when trying to handle their commercial and **lawful** (**private**) or **legal** (**public**) affairs.

In our society, the **private Strawman** was created by the application for the birth certificate; it is an *international vessel* in maritime law.

The **public STRAWMAN** was created by the application for the Social Security card; it is the *national vessel* in the law of admiralty.

John Doe is a *non-resident alien* in relation to the public. He exists in the *republic*. He has unalienable rights and unlimited liabilities.

JOHN DOE is a 14th Amendment U.S. citizen. He exists in the *democracy*. He has benefits and obligations and limited liability.

In the private, *money is an asset* and always in the form of something that has intrinsic value, i.e. gold or silver. Payment for anything is in the form of *commercial set off*, in the now.

In the public, *money is a liability* and normally in the form of a promissory note, i.e. an FRN, a check, a bond, or a note. Payment is in the form of *discharge;* in the future.

The private realm is the basis for all commcerce and contract; the public realm was created by the bankruptcy of the private entity. Generally, creditors operate from the private.

Public entities are all debtors (or slaves).

It is therefore, good to learn how to be a creditor in all of our affairs. Freedom is possible in the private; it is not possible in the public.

Creditor or Debtor?

Playing the game of commerce well means being a creditor, and not a debtor.

Debtors take positions, defend what they know, and make statements about it; they ignore, argue and/or contest as an aggressor always at war.

Extremely debtor-minded people presume victimhood and always seek to limit their liability.

Debtors unwittingly operate from and within the public domain. They are satisfied with only equitable title. They can supposedly own and operate on their terms, but not totally control their property. The Debtor's possibilities are limited and restrictive because debtors are slaves.

Creditors are present to whatever opportunity arises; they ask questions to bring remedy if called for; they accept responsibility either fully or conditionally. Accomplished creditors take full responsibility for their lives, their finances, and their world.

Creditors understand and utilize their unlimited ability to contract privately with anyone they choose at any time. They maintain legal title to, and control of their property. The Creditor's possibilities are infinite. Creditors are sovereign and free.

Produce the Note

There is a huge problem facing banks who are attempting to foreclose. Most of the original contract mortgage notes are not in their possession. Banks bundle up mortgage loans into packages, and sell and resell them to investors; and often, no one knows where they are or have ended up.

Facing a foreclosure, ahead of the court date, demand that the bank that is foreclosing on your property bring the **original signed note** to court. If the bank cannot produce the **original signed note** for any reason, the judge has to deny the foreclosure.

See: Brown: Landmark Decision promises massive relief for homeowners and trouble for banks, 9/19/9; Sixty Million Mortgages Kaput?; Produce the Note; Stay Put; How to make them Produce The Note

****

William Avery: Dispatch of Merchants
George Mercier: Invisible Contracts
Eustace Mullins: Secrets of the Federal Reserve
Mary Croft: How I Clobbered Every Bureaucratic ... Notes of Debt are not Income
Affidavit to Mr. Computer: http://www.scribd.com/doc/12965488/Affidavit-of-Truth-and-Fact-to-Mr-Computer
Real Money, Real Freedom: http://www.the7thfire.com/debt_elimination/Education.html

****

Re: Income Tax:

Why we have income tax; Is the Income Tax a Form of Slavery?; Taxation, Forced Labor & Theft; 31 Questions & Answers about the IRS; Debunking IRS Lies; IRS is Not An Agency of the US Government; Idiot Senator Majority Leader Harry Reid re: America's Voluntary Income Tax

Voluntary: http://dictionary.reference.com/browse/voluntary

^^^

One year odds of accidental death: 1 in 1,743; One year odds of IRS prosecution: 1 in 250,000:

http://trac.syr.edu/tracirs/findings/national/collenfG.html

One year odds of getting struck by lightening: 1 in 400,000:

http://www.lightningsafety.noaa.gov/medical.htm

Bevilacqua vs. Rodriguez

Massachusetts Attorney General Coakley Issues Statement on the SJC Decision in *Revilacqua vs. Rodriquez*

BOSTON – A decision by the Massachusetts Supreme Judicial Court (SJC) today in **Bevilacqua v. Rodriguez**, reaffirmed that a mortgage holder *must* have *both* "jurisdiction and authority" –a *valid* assignment of mortgage – in order to foreclose on a property.

Attorney General Martha Coakley issued the following statement: "This case is just one example of a much larger problem. In the rush to foreclose, the banks' reckless origination and foreclosure practices have created a domino effect that has harmed Massachusetts homeowners as well as third-party purchasers who purchased properties after foreclosure. This is yet another clear demonstration that the only way we are going to restore a healthy economy is to address the foreclosure crisis and hold the banks accountable for their actions."

BACKGROUND:

This case determined that because U.S. Bank *did not* hold a *valid* assignment of the mortgage at the time it initiated foreclosure proceedings, it *failed* to acquire title. As a result, not only did U.S. Bank foreclose *without* legal authority to do so, but its *failure* means that it was unable to transfer clear title to Mr. Bevilacqua.

As the SJC recently observed in *U.S. Bank, N.A. v. Ibanez*, many investors in the secondary mortgage market *ignored* longstanding requirements of Massachusetts law concerning when and how a mortgage ho*invalid* foreclosures.

Mr. Bevilacqua was a third-party purchaser of property that was foreclosed upon by U.S. Bank prior to the Land Court's initial decision in *Ibanez*. Mr. Rodriguez is the *prior* mortgagor. Because U.S. Bank *did not* hold a *valid* assignment *prior to* commencing foreclosure proceedings the foreclosure was deemed *invalid*. U.S. Bank foreclosed *without* legal authority and was *unable* to transfer clean title to Mr. Bevilacqua.

Bevilacqua brought an action under the so-called "try title" statute because the *Ibanez* decision had clouded Bevilaqua's claim to the property. It allows the holder of a clouded title to initiate an action to clear title *without* waiting for adverse claimants to sue *first*. The try title process provides that if *adequate* notice is issued and an adverse claimant *fails* to respond then the petitioner may obtain an order barring that claimant from *ever* challenging the petitioner's right to title.

The Land Court denied Bevilacqua's petition, ruling that one seeking to use the try title process must have at least a plausible claim to the title. The Court ruled that Bevilacqua has *no* such claim to title where he acquired a deed following an *invalid* foreclosure. The Land Court held that Bevilacqua acquired whatever it was that U.S. Bank had to sell as of the foreclosure. Because, per *Ibanez*, at the time of the foreclosure, the bank held *nothing*, Bevilacqua acquired *nothing* and had *no* standing as a result.

Today, the SJC affirmed the Land Court decision and reaffirmed the essential holdings of *Ibanez:* that the mortgage holder *must* have a *valid* assignment of mortgage in order to foreclose on a property. The Court also held that one cannot use the try title process to extinguish the right of redemption – a mortgagee can only foreclose by *strict adherence* to the statutory processes for foreclosure by exercising the power of sale or foreclosure by entry.

The Attorney General's Office filed an *amicus* brief in this case in April 2011 and presented oral arguments before the SJC on May 2, 2011.

Asset Protection

A DECLARATION TO RESTORE
THE CONSTITUTIONAL REPUBLIC

NATIONAL CALL FOR UNITED ACTION

A DECLARATION TO RESTORE THE CONSTITUTIONAL REPUBLIC

NATIONAL CALL FOR UNITED ACTION

(Circa. Oct. 1, 2011)

"When in the Course of human events it becomes necessary for one people to dissolve the political bands which have connected them with another and to assume among the powers of the earth, the separate and equal station to which the Laws of Nature and of Nature's God entitle them, a decent respect to the opinions of mankind requires that they should declare the causes which impel them to the separation."

"We hold these truths to be self-evident, that all men are created equal, that they are endowed by their Creator with certain unalienable Rights, that among these are Life, Liberty and the pursuit of Happiness. — That to secure these rights, Governments are instituted among Men, deriving their just powers from the consent of the governed, — That whenever any Form of Government becomes destructive of these ends, it is the Right of the People to alter or to abolish it, and to institute new Government, laying its foundation on such principles and organizing its powers in such form, as to them shall seem most likely to effect their Safety and Happiness." – [from the U.S. Declaration of Independence].

An undisclosed number of American Veterans and former service members have come together to prepare and present this Call-to-Action on behalf of the U.S. Constitution, the reseated Republic, the Rule of Law, and equal justice for all freedom loving citizens of the united States of America. Acting together as one, via The <u>Veteran Defenders of America</u>, co-sponsored by civilian patriot group <u>The United States Patriots Union</u>, LLC – we issue the following CALL for peaceful disobedience.

1. We CALL upon every member of federal, state and local government, legislative, judicial, law enforcement, and military, who have taken an oath to protect and defend the Constitutional Republic from all enemies, foreign and domestic, to act upon those oaths for the stated purpose of supporting the reinhabited Constitutional Republic.

2. We CALL upon ALL veterans and veteran organizations in America, who still believe in their oath to protect and defend, to unite with us at once - in this Declaration to Support the Constitutional Republic.

3. We CALL for ALL citizens who still desire freedom and liberty, to stand with us in peaceful protest, and carry our demands to right the wrongs against our nation in the preservation of freedom, liberty, justice and the rule of law.

This is a NATIONWIDE Call-to-Action!

"We are Facing a Battle That Will Decide our Fate as a Nation!" – Maj. Gen. Paul Vallely (Ret.)

The time to unite and fight for the American way of

life has arrived… We did not choose this fight, nor this time. The fight has come to us in our time and we will not shrink from our responsibility to protect and defend the United States of America, our Constitutional Republic and the American way of life. We CALL upon ALL freedom loving Americans to JOIN US in this honorable endeavor. We do so on the following basis…

Abuses and Usurpations

Barack Obama's once strong approval rating now stands at only 19%. The approval rating of congress is no better. The people have lost all faith in their government…

The demise of our Constitutional Republic has been underway for nearly a hundred years. As the people placidly accepted intolerable offenses against the republic, the states, and the Constitution for decades, the Central power in Washington D.C. grew ever more powerful, ever more abusive, and ever more disconnected from the very people it was formed to represent.

During the last three years, the current administration has committed the most egregious offenses against the people, the states, and the Constitution, since the founding of our country, and today they operate as a virtual dictatorship against the governed, beyond the scope and authority the people granted them in the Constitution, and at odds with the will of the vast majority of American citizens.

The actions of the Obama Administration, in total, rise to the level of treason against the United States and its people.

The <u>Democratic Socialists of America</u> are currently running Washington D.C. and they recently issued this statement in a Call-to-Action for their millions of members –

"We are the alternative to the tea party conservatives, the Republicans whose only program is to say No, the Democrats who have forgotten what progressive politics really are and the progressives who think that they can stand apart from the left."

This must not be permitted to stand...

Among other offenses, abuses and usurpations, is the following list of transgressions — (detailed in Appendix A) —   altering our constitutional form of government and system of justice without authority...

* Violations against Article I of the U.S. Constitution - Congress.

* Violations against Article II of the U.S. Constitution - The office of President.

* Violations against Article III of the U.S. Constitution - Judicial Powers.

* Volations against Article IV of the U.S. Constitution - The State.

* Violations against Article V of the U.S. Constitution - The Amendment Process.

* Violations against Article VI of the U.S. Constitution - Oath to the Constitution.

* Violations against the 1st Amendment of the Bill of Rights.

* Violations against the 2nd Amendment of the Bill of Rights.

* Violations against the 3rd Amendment of the Bill of Rights.

* Violations against the 4th Amendment of the Bill of Rights.

* Violations against the 5th Amendment of the Bill of Rights.

* Violations against the 6th Amendment of the Bill of Rights.

* Violations against the 7th Amendment of the Bill of Rights.

* Violations against the 8th Amendment of the Bill of Rights.

* Violations against the 9th Amendment of the Bill of Rights.

* Violations against the 10th Amendment of the Bill of Rights.

* Unlawful use of Military force, here and abroad.

* Violations of International Treaties and Laws.

* Numerous violations of the public trust.

* Misuse of the people's resources.

* The bankrupting of the nation, the states and the people.

* Taxation without representation.

* Confiscation and Redistribution of the people's earned assets.

* Abuse of Judicial power.

At this late date, the individually itemized list of abuses and usurpations would require an encyclopedia of unconstitutional offenses to the Republic and there is no evidence to suggest that there remains even one legitimate honest courtroom in the country to which all evidence could be presented.

There is no Article or Amendment of the U.S. Constitution which the current leadership in Washington D.C. has not abused and/or usurped over the last three years.

As a result, the normal courses of action for redress may not be adequate to solve the problem today, as all three branches of the federal government are currently acting as one, all of them beyond the scope and power granted them by the Constitution, against the principles of freedom, liberty and self-governance, and at odds with the vast majority of citizens.

Yet the Constitutional Representative Republic must be restored, no matter the means or the cost.

It is on this foundation that we morally and rightfully call for all good people to rise up, stand together, move to restore the Constitutional Republic, and hold those who have and would stand against the people, fully accountable.

WE THE PEOPLE

On behalf of the Veterans and former Service Members of America, who fought and died for freedom and liberty here and abroad, and all good and decent American citizens from sea to shining sea, we the people of the United States of America hereby demand the immediate restoration of our Constitutional Republic and an end to the Democratic Socialist abuses and usurpations which have become commonplace in the daily corruption of our governmental offices. As the true American people sit idle, the enemy grows in number and strength.

No longer will we sit idly by and tolerate the utter destruction of our country, at the hands of anti-American elitists in Washington D.C. who have mistaken the people's peaceful tolerance for acceptance of their ill-advised behaviors. The time for all good and decent Americans to stand together, in defense of the Constitution, the Republic, freedom and liberty, has arrived. The Rule of Constitutional Law must prevail. We call upon all who have taken an oath to protect and defend, to take appropriate measures now.

We the people hereby demand

1. The immediate and unconditional and orderly resignation of Barack Hussein Obama, II.

2. The immediate and unconditional and orderly resignation of Joseph R. Biden.

In addition to the known fact that the Obama/Biden ticket was advanced by way of fraudulent representations concerning the constitutional eligibility of Barack Hussein Obama II, under Article II requirements for the office of President, the Obama/Biden has committed countless crimes against the U.S. Constitution, our Republican form of government, and the American people, while in control of the Executive Branch.

They are not able to do this alone, but with the help and cover of many anti-American players, who have also acted at odds with their oaths to protect and defend the Constitution, our Republic, and the people of the United States. As a result, these players must be removed from office and held accountable for their actions as well.

This group includes, but is not limited to the following individuals -

1. The immediate unconditional and orderly resignation of the entire Obama Cabinet, including but not limited to;

   * the White House staff and unelected Czar's.

   * Secretary of State Hillary Rodham Clinton.

   * Treasury Secretary Timothy F. Geithner.

   * Defense Secretary Leon E. Panetta.

   * Attorney General Eric H. Holder, Jr..

   * Interior Secretary Kenneth L. Salazar.

   * Acting Commerce Secretary Dr. Rebecca M. Blank.

   * Labor Secretary Hilda L. Solis.

   * Health and Human Services Secretary Kathleen Sebelius.

* Energy Secretary Steven Chu.

* Education Secretary Arne Duncan.

* Homeland Security Secretary Janet A. Napolitano.

* EPA Administrator Lisa P. Jackson.

* Office of Management & Budget Director Jacob J. Lew.

* UN Ambassador Susan Rice, and the entire Council of Economic Advisers.

* Supreme Court Justice Elena Kagan.

* Supreme Court Justice Sonia Sotomayor.

* House Speaker John Boehner.

* House Minority Leader Nancy Pelosi.

* Senate Leader Harry Reid.

* Senate Minority Leader Mitch McConnell.

All of whom have committed treasonous acts against the people, the states and the U.S. Constitution.

Further, to reinstate the rule of law and the Law of this Land, the U.S. Constitution and our constitutional republic -

1. In compliance with Article II – Section I of the U.S. Constitution for the Removal of the President from Office, or of his Death, Resignation, or Inability to discharge the Powers and Duties of the said Office, the Same shall devolve on the Vice President, — the Congress may by Law provide for the Case of Removal,

Death, Resignation or Inability, both of the President and Vice President, declaring what Officer shall then act as President, and such Officer shall act accordingly, until the Disability be removed, or a President shall be elected.

2. That every verifiable member of The Communist Party USA, The Socialist Party USA, and The Democratic Socialists of America, be immediately publicly identified and removed from office for overtly acting against freedom, liberty, and the Constitutional Republic.

3. That in the event that these individuals refuse to immediately resign in an orderly fashion designed to serve the best interests of the United States, we demand that the 66 members of the people's House who voted against the recent raising of the nation's debt ceiling, to immediately begin impeachment proceedings against every member of the Obama administration.

4. That the seven remaining members of the U.S. Supreme Court place an immediate stay on all Executive and Legislative actions taken under the term of the unconstitutional administration beginning January 20, 2009.

5. That remaining members of the House and Senate immediately act to name new majority and minority leaders of congress, and work with the U.S. Supreme Court in the assigning of new temporary Executive Branch members, acting on behalf of the people and the will of the American majority until such time that the citizens of the United States can elect their new representatives in 2012.

6. The immediate and unconditional dissolution of all special interest congressional caucuses, including but

not limited to The Progressive Caucus, The Black Caucus. In addition, the immediate closure of any and all congressional committees which have been given unconstitutional powers, including the Debt Committee of twelve just formed. Individuals are elected by the people to represent ALL of the people, not special interest groups.

7. That each state government immediately act to enforce its 10th Amendment right to protect and defend the people of their state against a tyrannical central power in Washington D.C., by recalling all State Guard troops home to protect the sovereignty and security of their respective citizens, as well as state resources and governments.

8. That each state government act immediately to cut itself off from federal funding, and take the necessary actions to balance their own state and local budgets immediately.

These are our initial demands and nothing less than complete compliance with each of these demands is acceptable to the people of the United States. These demands have been published for public support and delivered to all members of Congress.

Further, it is our position that the normal constitutional line of succession to the presidency does not apply in this circumstance, due to the widespread complicity by members of congress, regarding both the original fraud that placed this administration in power and the ongoing effort to cover up the greatest fraud ever perpetrated on the

American citizens.

The abuse and usurpation of the U.S. Constitution will not be allowed to stand. It is on this basis that We the People make these demands, in full compliance with the law of this land, the Constitution of the United States of America.

It is our sincere desire to affect these immediate and unconditional changes to the people's government through peaceful processes, causing a minimum degree of disruption to the vital ongoing business of the people and their representative government.

The individuals named in our demand for immediate and unconditional resignations have acted directly and overtly against the people, the states and the Constitution and they must be held fully accountable for their actions.

Call for the People to ACT Now

We are openly for the American people to draw a final line in the sand and take a moral and righteous stand for the Constitutional Republic, the rule of law and the future of freedom and liberty.

The time to be tolerant and silent has passed and the time for serious action has arrived. Only the people can restore the Constitution as the Supreme Law of this Land. We must do it peacefully, if at all possible, and our Founders provided all the tools necessary for peaceful corrections of a ship set off course by internal enemies.

We are calling for the following specific actions, by

every active and former service member, and every patriotic citizen, no matter their political stripe...

* We call upon all members of the U.S. Military, the U.S. Supreme Court, Federal, State, County, Local Law Enforcement, and all Intelligence agencies, to direct all assets of the people of the United States towards the restoration of the Constitutional Republic and stand with the American citizens in compliance with their oath to protect and defend the U.S. Constitution and the people of the United States.

* **We call upon ALL American citizens** to provide necessary pressure on all law enforcement, judicial, intelligence, and military agencies, until those who have sworn to protect and defend the Constitution begin to act upon those oaths.

* The current administration has done all it can to whip racial tensions and class warfare into full-blown riots and civil war, including scheduling a "U.S. Day of Rage" for communists, labor union socialists, illegal immigrants, Muslims, and blacks across the country. Their "Day of Rage" was scheduled for Constitution Day, September 17, 2011, and although it was a total flop, they will continue to rage against America. It is an open assault on free-market capitalism, waged by modern day Marxists who must be stripped of their entitlement mentality. The LEFT is also planning a *"Cairo style occupation of Washington in October, on the ground, on Wall Street now, and headed towards Washington D.C."* These events are being run by the Obama White House, via a number of left-wing front organizations.

* We The Veteran Defenders of America and The United States Patriots Union call for a "unified march" from ALL fifty (50) states to Washington D.C. on Friday November 11, 2011, Veterans Day — The Veterans March on D.C. Day — In defense of freedom, liberty and justice — led by American veterans and former service members with a clear purpose to demand the immediate restoration of the U.S. Constitution, the removal and prosecution of all of the individuals named herein; by voluntary resignation or articles of impeachment; and the end to Sharia Law on American soil.

* We call for all Americans who truly do support our troops to march on D.C., with our veterans. We call upon ALL independent truckers, independent contractors, all non-union workers, all independent business owners, agents and investors, all who support free-market capitalism and the right to work, earn and own, to march together with our veterans and former service members on November 11, 2011 – Veterans Day!

* To be prepared to act as citizens to protect and preserve the Constitutional Republic, in the event that our public servants, who have sworn an oath to the Constitutional Republic, refuse, for any reason, to act upon those oaths.

* To act peacefully, but prepared for a violent reaction from our nation's enemies. To avoid if possible, the RACE WAR being incited by the Obama Administration and the Black and Progressive Caucus's.

* Locally, to confront all anti-American infringements upon our Natural Rights, with boots on the ground when-

ever and wherever local, state or federal officials act beyond their scope of authority, or at odds with the Constitutional Rights of the people.

* To begin to openly identify and address government corruption at the local, county, and state levels, too often found in both governmental and law enforcement offices, also sworn to protect and serve the people of the United States.

* To be ready and willing to end the taxation without real representation, by refusing to fund the anti-American regime currently in control of Washington D.C., until such time as the taxpayers of this nation are once again properly represented.

* To make the necessary provisions to secure and protect your families and neighborhoods in the event of economic instability and social chaos, similar to events already witnessed abroad, by stocking up on cash, food and water supplies, as well as personal protection items.

* In the event that the current administration, or its thuggish supporters, attempt to use government or civilian force and violence to silence the people — as in the cases of Syria, Libya, Yemen, China's Tiananmen Square, the Bonus Army of 1932 in the United States, or the UK presently wrestling with black and Muslim violence — the people must be prepared to defend themselves against such tyrannical tactics. We cannot expect that the federal government will act in the best interest of American veterans or citizens.

This CALL FOR ACTION is being issued as a joint initiative, by the leaders and members of The Veteran Defenders of America, The United States Patriots Union. All citizens who want to see the Constitutional Republic restored immediately are encouraged to immediately join one of these unified organizations and become directly engaged in our joint missions to restore America to that shining city on a hill, and beacon of freedom and liberty around the world. We the People are the solution!

Volunteer leaders across the country must join one of these organizations to take part in leading in their local areas. All supporters who do not wish to join these organizations but who do support the initiative can keep up with information concerning the action here.

Foundation for Our United Action

Our Declaration of 1776 establishes the principles upon which The United States of America was founded. On September 17, 1787, our nation's Founders ratified The United States Constitution, forming a Constitutional Representative Republic as our system of self-governance. From that day forward, the American people are guaranteed a Constitutional Representative Republic, of, by and for the people, which was to operate, at all times, within the confines of the limited authority provided the government by the people and their states.

For decades, our federal government has been operating beyond its constitutional authority, infringing upon the Natural Rights of every American citizen, and every American enterprise, until our government has indeed become destructive of the common cause of freedom and liberty.

In its usurpations of the Constitution, it has committed atrocities against the people for whom it was designed to protect and serve, until the people are forced to rise up in the name of freedom and liberty, casting off the shackles of soft tyranny, and it is the Right of the People to alter or to abolish it, and to institute new Government, laying its foundation on such principles and organizing its powers in such form, as to them shall seem most likely to effect their Safety and Happiness.

"When a long train of abuses and usurpations, pursuing invariably the same Object evinces a design to reduce them under absolute Despotism, it is their right, it is their duty, to throw off such Government, and to provide new Guards for their future security."

Our United Mission

We are finished with changing America to suit every anti-American whim… This time, the change is coming to Washington D.C.

It is not our intent to separate from any foreign King, nor to abolish or alter our Constitutional Representative Republic, but rather to restore it, as the Supreme law of this land, under which both the government and the governed must live.

Our united mission is to end the march of democratic socialism, which has become the most dangerous modern threat to American peace, prosperity, freedom and liberty and reinstate the republican form of self-governance guaranteed every citizen in the U.S. Constitution.

To accomplish this objective, the people responsible for the usurpation of the Constitution must be immediately removed from office and held fully accountable for their actions, setting an example for future generations, who must also be forever vigilant in the common defense of freedom and liberty.

The long train of abuses and usurpations must be brought to a swift end and the Constitutional Republic must prevail, or the United States of America will soon cease to exist.

Our mission is just – it is moral – it is legal and constitutional, and it is necessary...

This is not a call to overthrow our entire institutions of government, or subvert the Law of the Land, but rather to restore those institutions to their honorable constitutional forms. As such, and under their oaths to the Constitution and the people whom they are sworn to protect and defend against all enemies, foreign and domestic, it is incumbent upon every citizen, veteran, soldier, officer, and agent, to use the tools of the people to protect the people and return our government to a Constitutional Republic, of, by, and for the people.

Let Freedom Ring! May the Creator, who endowed each of us with certain unalienable rights, among them the right to Life, Liberty, and the individual Pursuit of Happiness, free from government tyranny, bless this mission, of, by and for, the people of the United States, and may the Lord let freedom ring in America, once again.

We demand an end to government corruption, an end to despotic leadership in D.C., an end to the current assault on all decent and honest American taxpayers, businesses, and   honorable public servants of the people.

We demand the peaceful return of the people's government, and we will remain resolute in the defense of the Constitution, and the United States of America, until the people can once again, feel secure in their nation and government.

IN GOD WE TRUST!

JOIN the MISSION HERE -
http://www.veterandefenders.org/
or HERE -
http://www.patriotsunion.org/
Non-members can follow the mission here -
http://www.facebook.com/groups/262343767138128/

APPENDIX "A"

As a preface to APPENDIX "A", the following items only scratch the surface. The blatant abrogation of the United States Constitution, trampling the boundaries of law-based authority, deceit, bribery, aiding and abetting our sworn enemies, illegal manipulation of our election process, and subverting election laws, and hundreds of other affronts and assaults to our liberties and freedoms, all fall under the category of "high crimes and misdemeanors."

1. Obama is a National Security threat since he definitely has questionable allegiance to the United States, not to mention his refusal to complete and release full, frank and truthful answers as to who he is. Obama has demonstrated a blatant disregard for the public safety and security.

2. Obama and his handlers released an obvious forged birth certificate after releasing at least two fraudulent COLBs (Certifications of Live Birth). Obama is also using numerous stolen Social Security numbers.

3. Obama and his incompetent advisors have wreaked economic tyranny on the American people, all the while calling for the rest of us to endure economic sacrifice.

4. Obama has destroyed accepted administrative process by creating 32 Czars who only report to him, bypassing the Congress and Cabinet. *

5. In one year, Obama and his minions doubled our national debt, which took 200 years to accumulate.

6. Obama and his Justice Department sided with a foreign government (Mexico) when they sued the State of Arizona in order to force the continuation of illegal immigration. *

7. Obama and his henchmen proposed a 1% tax on all bank transactions (HR4646) to be implemented after the November 2012 elections.

8. Obama signed HB1388 to use $20 million in taxpayer money to immigrate Hamas refugees to USA, and other migration assistance to Palestinian refugees.

9. Obama passed "Dream Act" by Executive Order which aide's illegal aliens through "prosecutorial discretion" all to garner votes for his election. The Heritage Foundation has provided extensive proof that illegal aliens and immigrants with green cards are committing rampant voter fraud. *

10. Obama's socialist, radical, dictatorial Moratorium on drilling in the Gulf of Mexico, for thirty years a major source of energy for America, and which a Federal Court ruled was unconstitutional, continues to prevent drilling, all under the pretense to protect the environment and the fraudulent notion of global warming. He is indifferent to the loss of 10,000 jobs, and 87,000 workers, destroyed. Perfect excuse to push "Cap and Trade" with environmental regulations, and to push for governmental control of energy industries, i.e. General Motors, banking and healthcare.

11. Obama and his Czars want to tax church contributions and replace charities with government welfare. *

12. This administrations massive expansion of the federal government (350,000 employees) through agencies and Czars, whose goal is to "fundamentally transform America."

13. Obama's own Federal Elections Commission documented that he got at least $33.8 million from disallowed foreign contributions, including 520 contributions from interests in Iran, and $30,000 from Hamas-controlled Gaza area. *

14. Obama said, "We must reward our friends and

punish our enemies." 70 individuals who raised $50,000 or more for him "have been rewarded with ambassadorships or high Ranking jobs."

15. Obama and the cabal's National Security Strategy released in May, allows for the targeted assassination of US citizens including "homegrown terrorists" without due process. *

16. Obama dhimmitude given Ramadan and Iftar dinners in the White House, while he cancels the National Day of Prayer without one word of objection from the Congress.

17. Obama and his Muslim buddies agree and defend a 15 story mosque, bankrolled by terrorist sympathizers and anti-American Muslim groups, to be erected feet from the hallowed ground of the World Trade Center.

18. Obama and his Justice Department's refusal to support, defend and enforce US law, i.e. Defense of Marriage Act, stating it was unconstitutional, thereby circumventing established law and the rulings of the courts. *

19. Obama and his warmongers attack Libya without any authority from Congress. *

20. ObamaCare ruled unconstitutional and ordered stopped by the Federal Court…it was implemented regardless of the Federal Court. *

21. Congress said Cap and Trade was unconstitutional and refused to pass the same. Obama ordered the EPA to enact the provisions regardless of the Congressional ruling. *

22. Obama's use of taxpayer money to pay for Democrat propaganda including $15 million for The American Reinvestment and Recovery Act road signs and $18 million for the continually misleading recovery.gov website.
*

23. $770 million of taxpayer funds given to Egypt and Cyprus for the restoration of mosques through USAID. *

24. Obama has disgraced the United States by bowing to foreign potentates, while at the same time snubbed our longtime allies, Great Britain and Israel. Obama and his friends have deliberately fostered hate against the Jews and Israel by promoting a Palestinian State.

25. Obama's Department of Justice, refusing to prosecute Black Panthers in Philadelphia caught on tape brandishing weapons in front of a voting site to intimidate voters. Further the stated intentions of political appointees of Obama who said they would ignore voter crimes committed by blacks, Latinos, and other minorities. *

26. Obama and his Cabinet intentionally refusing to secure our nation's borders is in direct violation of Article IV, Section 4 of the Constitution. This is an effort to blackmail Republican support for comprehensive immigration reform. They are in essence holding the Border States and residents as political hostages during a time when they live in fear and danger. *

27. Obama and his handlers continually ignore Congress's constitutional obligation to vet presidential appointees, as none of his 32 Czars was vetted by Congress, and his appointment of the head of the Centers

for Medicare and Medicaid Services was appointed during Congress recess. *

28. Department of Homeland Security now investigating to determine the political association for those making Freedom of Information Act Requests. If you are a Republican, your request will be delayed, and even ignored altogether.

29. Obama's Justice Department refusing to sue sanctuary cities for violating US immigration law. *

30. Obama's executive order which allows Interpol to operate in the US with no restraints, and without any oversight from Congress, courts, FBI, or local law enforcement. *

31. Obama's administration and Justice Department discourage whistleblowers, and prosecute them.

32. Secretary Of State Hillary Clinton's ongoing effort to create international small arms accords that will subvert the Second Amendment rights of US citizens.

33. Obama and his State Department has failed to treat as an Act of War the takeover of sovereign land belonging to Arizona by the Mexican drug cartel.

34. The State Department used $23 million in taxpayer money to transform Kenya into a constitutionally communist country where freedom of speech is limited and property rights are based on social justice. Don't forget the Kenyan constitution allows for Sharia Law in some regions, which means women will not have basic human rights. *

35. As part of the auto industry bailout and forced closings, shut down an unbelievable disproportionate number of dealerships in rural areas that did not vote for Obama.

36. Obama's refusal to have a press conference and answer the difficult questions as is expected by every US President. And as is usual...with his total lack of respect for anyone but himself...he is always late for everything.

37. Obama and his minions have downgraded the value of human life with their opposition to his signing "Born Alive Infants Protection Act"; however they lifted the ban on overseas abortion funding using US taxpayer's money.

38. Obama's State Department foreign policy continually will do anything to insult our allies, embarrass the United States, all the while elevating and promoting third world Muslim countries.*

39. Obama and his environmentalist henchmen are prohibiting US industries from taking advantage of our own natural resources including coal, oil, uranium and timber. *

40. Despite all the political rhetoric about the historical downgrade of our nation's credit rating, the devaluation was a mere shadow of the colossal degradation Obama and his socialist cadres have inflicted on our Country since January 20, 2009. More significant than our nation's credit, our nation's credibility as a constitutional republic has suffered relentless and ruthless dam-

age and offense. *

41. Obama deployed 1200 National Guard troops to Border States, where they will, under no circumstances, be used to stop the flow of illegal aliens and drug traffickers.

42. Despite a court's ruling and Congress's opposition, Obama's FCC continues to try to gain control over the Internet, by reclassifying internet companies as telecommunications providers, thereby making them subject to FCC regulation. *

43. A slick move no one noticed, moving the Census Bureau out of the Commerce Department directly into the White House and under the control and management of Rahm Emmanuel, Chief of Staff.

44. Obama attempts to run this Country with Executive Orders.

45. Under the cover of secrecy, and without any input from Congress, state, or local officials, and current land owners, the Department of the Interior plans to take control of millions of public and private lands in Western states by designating them as national monuments.

46. Obama through Eric Holder has handcuffed and taken over the CIA, which has been the most critical, independent information gathering resource safe-guarding our national security. Obama has revealed, ridiculed, and condemned CIA interrogation methods which were previously approved by Congress and cleared through the Justice Department. He has demonstrated, to our enemies (terrorists), that they need not fear us. *

47. Obama's known history is replete with symbiotic associations and participation with admitted anti-American radicals, many of which/who advocate the destruction of American imperialism and capitalism, even through violent means. Consider William Ayers, Khalid Al Mansour, Rhashid Khalidi, Jeremiah Wright, Sol Alinsky, James Cone, Mike Klonsky, as well as organizations such as the Weather Underground, STORM, Chicago Annenberg Challenge, Woods Foundation, ACORN, which have all received major tax payer funded support. Obama has never denied or even argued about his nefarious involvement with these people and organizations.

48. At the expense of the American taxpayer, to the tune of $6 Billion, Obama and his handlers have established their own Civilian Paramilitary Security Force, made up with the likes of SEIU, STORM, ACORN, RUCKUS, The Apollo Project (Soros), AmeriCorps, Color of Change, Drummond Pike/Project, and others who choose to remain anonymous. *

49. Loss of free speech, to the tune of half a billion dollars of taxpayer money, given to Obama appointee Mark Lloyd "FCC Diversity Officer", and avowed pro-Chavez radical, ordered by Obama to rein in free speech on the airwaves by reorganizing the FCC and placing a tax equal to the annual operating costs on local radio stations, which they either pay or lose their license to a new minority owner. *

50. Historic and unprecedented move by Obama's cabal to indoctrinate our children in socialist, humanist garbage, sent a video to all schools, and naturally this

scheme was promoted by the NEA, with the children taking a pledge, *"...to be a servant to our president and to all mankind"*, and then they chant over and over *"together we can."* He is asking our children to choose him and his agenda, over anything you might teach at home.
*

51. Obama's appointment of Safe Schools Czar, Kevin Jennings, founder of Gay, Lesbian & Straight Education Network, has determined "required reading material" for our schools, which promotes pornography, not to mention homosexuality. This information is so massive, if you type into Google, Obama's "Safe Schools Czar" Is Promoting Child Porn in the classroom — Kevin Jennings and the GLSEN Reading List, click on the first site, you can read it for yourself...be prepared to vomit. *

52. Obama protected union interests over those of GM and Chrysler bond holders during bankruptcy proceedings, forcing investors to accept millions in losses, funds which they were legally entitled to. *

53. In a time when Americans are asked to sacrifice, I guess this does not apply to Michelle Obama, since she has 22 personal assistants, which does not include a markup artist and hair stylist, at the cost to the American taxpayer of $6,364,000 for 4 years. These assistants' sole duties are to facilitate her social life. She must be a lot more incompetent than first thought, since as First Ladies Hillary Clinton only had 3 assistants, Jacqueline Kennedy had 1 assistant, and Laura Bush had 1 assistant.

54. On June 9, 2011, Obama signed Executive Order 13575 establishing the "White House Rural Council" which establishes unchecked federal control into rural America in education, food supply, land use, water use, recreation, property, energy, and the lives of 16% of the US population. No Congressional or local government oversight or input. *

55. Obama's handler's establishment of the "Super Committee" is the final nail in our republic's coffin, and the establishment of a Marxist dictatorship. Congress has always had committees which meet and return to the main body with ideas and suggestions, which is then amended, debated, rewritten, and finally voted on. Not this Super Committee, their determinations are presented to the Congress who are not allowed to discuss debate, modify, rewrite. The Congress is limited to a straight up or down vote. Why is the Congress accepting this infringement on their constitutional duties? *

56. Obama forced British Petroleum to set up $20 billion slush fund supposedly to compensate Gulf coast residents and businesses, and sets up an Obama appointee to administer funds with no judicial or congressional oversight. *

57. Obama's cabal cancelled 77 oil field development contracts already certified as proper by the Bush administration. This deliberate affront by Obama's Interior Secretary prevents the extraction of 3 trillion gallons of oil in Colorado, Utah, Wyoming and North Dakota, which is more than enough to end our dependence on foreign oil. *

58. Obama signed the Russian-American START treaty which hampers US missile defense development and makes it difficult for us to modernize our rapidly aging nuclear weapons arsenal. It represents unilateral disarmament by the US in return for nothing more than Russian good will. What a joke.

59. Perhaps one of Obama's most pathetic stunts was his chair of the UN Security Council, never done by a US sitting President. He was in the right place sitting as chair over an organization ruled by tyrants, and showing his true dual loyalties.

60. We need to look at Obama's character, or in this case, his lack thereof. Obama is a total incognito with zero accomplishments. No experience, no education, no business sense or experience (only 8% of his entire administration has ever held a real job or run a business, other than being on the government dole), no military experience, a dangerous and treacherous narcissist, arrogant, incompetent, no class, serial liar, no humility, juvenile, no dignity, no genuine empathy, his personal narcissism and arrogance, veiled by his hollow spoken empathy, quite ignorant, racist, Muslim, bereft of conscience, unable to determine between his fantasy and reality, incapable of genuine caring or concern, artificial, blames everyone else for his failure, and most of all Obama is a puppet, owned by his handlers, who maneuvered and manufactured his pathetic life.

61. Misuse of federal power and money in illegal international gun and drug running, the mis-distribution of taxpayer funds and manipulation of foreign governments,

racketeering and smuggling, such as <u>Project Gun Runner,</u> resulting in the murder of U.S. agents.

NOTE: The items herein marked with an (*) at the end of the numbered statement, reflect a deliberate and malicious violation of the duties of the President as cited in Article II, Section 3. Of the United States Constitution, i.e. *"...he shall take care that the laws be faithfully executed...".*

Asset Protection

NESARA: National *Economic Security and Reformation Act*
http://tinyurl.com/c8u42q6

History of Banking: *An Asian Perspective*
http://tinyurl.com/boeehjl

The People's Voice: *Former Arizona Sheriff Richard Mack*
http://tinyurl.com/d62fyg3

Asset Protection: *Pure Trust Organizations*
http://tinyurl.com/btrjfqp

The Matrix As It Is: *A Different Point Of View*
http://tinyurl.com/ckrbkge

From Debt To Prosperity: *'Social Credit' Defined*
http://tinyurl.com/d2tjmw3

Give Yourself Credit: *Money Doesn't Grow On Trees*
http://tinyurl.com/d7tphuv

My Home Is My Castle: *Beware Of The Dog*
http://tinyurl.com/bmzxc2n

Commercial Redemption: *The Hidden Truth*
http://tinyurl.com/d9etg7w

Hardcore Redemption-In-Law: *Commercial Freedom And Release*
http://tinyurl.com/cl65vrz

Oil Beneath Our Feet: *America's Energy Non-Crisis*
http://tinyurl.com/btlzqxf

Untold History Of America: *Let The Truth Be Told*
http://tinyurl.com/bu9kjjc

Debtocracy: *& Odious Debt Explained*
http://tinyurl.com/cooqzuz

New Beginning Study Course: *Connect The Dots And See*
http://tinyurl.com/cxpk42p

Monitions of a Mountain Man: *Manna, Money, & Me*
http://tinyurl.com/cusgcqs

Maine Street Miracle: *Saving Yourself And America*
http://tinyurl.com/d4yktlw

Reclaim Your Sovereignty: *Take Back Your Christian Name*
http://tinyurl.com/cf5taxh

Gun Carry In The USA: Your Right To Self-defence
http://tinyurl.com/cdn3y3y

Climategate Debunked: *Big Brother, Main Stream Media*
http://tinyurl.com/d6gy2xz

Epistle to the Americans I: *What you don't
know about The Income Tax*
http://tinyurl.com/d99ujzm

Epistle to the Americans II: *What you don't
know about American History*
http://tinyurl.com/cnyghyz

Epistle to the Americans III: *What you don't
know about Money*
http://tinyurl.com/cp8nrh8